Reflections in a
Writer's Eye

Reflections in a Writer's Eye

Travel Pieces by
ANGUS WILSON

*
*   *
*

Secker & Warburg
LONDON

First published in a one-volume edition in 1986
by Martin Secker & Warburg Limited
54 Poland Street, London W1V 3DF

British Library Cataloguing in Publication Data
Wilson, Angus, *1913–*
   Reflections in a writer's eye.
   1. Voyages and travels—1951–
   I. Title
   910.4   G465

ISBN 0-436-57611-2

Set in 11/13 pt Linotron Baskerville by
Hewer Text Composition Services, Edinburgh
Printed by Redwood Burn Ltd
Trowbridge, Wiltshire

For my friend Jaidev

Contents

Introduction

Travel was not an activity which played much part in my childhood life. I was born a year before the First World War broke out, on the South Coast at Bexhill, in Sussex. My parents exulted with pride each time they thought themselves to have heard gunfire from across the Channel, where three of their six sons fought for long periods at the front line. My front line was on the English side – all my days were spent on the rocks, catching crabs and decorating myself in seaweed. I never heard any gunfire to the embarrassment of the more patriotic friends of my parents.

Despite our coastal existence, none of my brothers was in the Navy, yet it was this unlikely force that commanded my four- and five-year-old allegiance (indeed, this lasted up to my eleventh year when the glories of the war were well over). I remembered these naval ambitions into later years, but, by my twelfth year I had rejected such memories as a spurious delusion. How could I have nourished naval ambitions when I remembered so clearly my childhood arguments with myself as to whether I should have made a better Royal mistress as Madame de Montespan or as Lady Castlemaine (these were my two preferred King's ladies – not too clever like Madame de Maintenon, not too popular like Nell Gwynne)? It is only in the last few years that, going over old photographs, I began to suspect that my early naval ambitions were not so illusory. Many times I came upon myself in naval uniform making a sailor's

1

salute (careful as I always was in childhood to preserve my dear little Peter Pan appearance, even in martial guise). No, a sailor I wished to be – until adolescence brought me more sophisticated, more worldly ambitions – for the stage and for a professorship. 'Scholarships, not battleships' was my pacifist cry at sixteen years, but at nine years it was just ships and a uniform which made up the world of my ambitions.

In 1922 we travelled to South Africa for a two-year stay in Durban. This journey to my Mother's home country was the only real travel of my early years. The journey on the Union Castle liner to South Africa was certainly an experience that really did re-shape my outlook with its strange novelties – Afrikaans speech, meals of delicious mealies, and even, as we neared Cape Town, of pineapples and mangoes. Even more dislodging from the old Johnstone-Wilson life was our return journey to England on an Australian liner of the Blue Funnel Company. Here I made (and had to make) many friends among Australian boys and girls. Their intelligence and liveliness were to prepare me for the welcome reception of my visit to Australia about fifty years later.

Through all this dream of travel and boats, mixtures of colonialism, strange food and talk of African wildlife (hippos and giraffes), I remained contained by my close family life. My favourite reading was *The Swiss Family Robinson*, not *Robinson Crusoe* (that was the book reserved to prepare future readers for the more transcendent solitude of William Golding's wonderful world). There were few human strangenesses that I associate with this boyhood travel to South Africa and back. Life on the *Dunluce Castle* was a prologue not to adventure or self-discovery, but to the disintegrating middle-class world of private hotels which was to be the background of my public school years at Westminster. As to Durban (and we went hardly anywhere else after we got to South Africa) it vastly increased 'the family', with its aunts and cousins whom, like Sir Joseph Porter in *HMS Pinafore* – a part I was later to play in school – I reckoned up by dozens. It certainly destroyed for me any worry about colour that I had acquired from my early childhood friends of Raj background. Indeed, the happiest of my memories of Durban were of the two successive black servants whom we called 'boys', and whom I, with my persistent passion for history language, called the two Georges. They were our two Zulu house servants. I sat on their knees and listened to their stories of how the Zulus had killed the King of France (in fact, the Prince Imperial, Napoleon the Third's son, who was killed in the Zulu War). In conversation when we got back to England, I repeated these boasts to the evident embarrassment and dislike of the English men and women who were our co-residents in Kensington hotels.

One concrete and very good result was when, thirty years later, I came by chance to read Kipling's reminiscences of his happy Bombay childhood with his Ayah and his bearer, it was so much my own happy experience with the two Georges that I became a Kipling devotee. As I said goodbye in turn to the two Georges on a jetty that led into Durban bay (of course, no Kaffir could come into the Durban hotel in which we spent our last South African days) I little knew that it was a preface to many months of happy travelling, many years later, in the North and West of India collecting material for the biography I wrote of Kipling. A wonderful illustration of the adventitious nature of foreign travel.

All this was the small measure of my knowledge of 'abroad' when I was still a boy. In my prep school years I went abroad very little. The headmaster of the school was my second brother – the most excellent member of my family in humour, reading, and athletics. But also, perhaps because he had been severely wounded twice in France, the most insular of them all. His wife said, I remember, with conviction, 'Oh yes, Paris is nice, but so is Brighton.' My parents took me to Boulogne, where I was characteristically drawn to love of France by the praise of my Charleston dancing by the professional couple who managed the ballroom in the Casino. And I visited the American parents of a friend who lived in The Hague, and saw there paintings in

3

the Mauritshuis but it was no eye-opener to the wonders of paintings which so enlarged my vision in my adult years. It was more useful in teasing my Mother, who was delighted by my characteristic, as she believed, taste for the unusual – Ruysdael, rather than the dreary overpraised Rembrandt. I was pleased to have pleased her. Already, with American friends to visit in Holland, I was beginning to feel guilty about the breadth of my life compared to hers. In 1929 my Mother died, and all things changed. Gradually I began to travel in the wake of my third brother and his French wife. It was agreed that at fifteen I should visit her Mother in La Ciotat in Southern France, on my own.

The thirties strengthened my ties with France, for, like a very large percentage of young English, my sympathies were strongly anti-fascist. With no Germany, Italy, Spain or Portugal, France alone could be visited. Although, when I come to think of it, many of my contemporaries at Oxford, and later on the Staff of the British Museum, had spent time in Hitler's Germany. Was I more realistic or idealistic? I truly don't know. At any rate I was very consistent in my anti-fascism, so that quite recently in Portugal I received a tremendous shock when an attractive young Frenchman, whom I was very flattered to find flirtatious with me (at my age!), said suddenly, 'Oh, Angus, tu n'es pas fasciste? Comme ça me fait triste!'

But in the twenty years between 1930 and 1950 it was France (and France as a whole) that stood for abroad for me. Starting with the Midi, and gradually including almost every part. My sense of the nature of sexual licence (a particularly absurd thing when I reflect on the easy indifferent tolerance the French, I believe, have towards homosexual life – but then I was a literary young man and inevitably Proust and Gide counted for so much for me), was sharpened and enriched there. My taste for food, of course, as much so if not more. My discrimination of architectural beauty became increasingly compulsive as my knowledge of France's cathedrals grew with my travels. Above all, it was French cafés and French crowds that sharpened my ear for the conversation of strangers: in some way the most important contribution that travel can make for a future novelist or playwright. Anyway, it was there in France that my passion for travel grew until the French frontier began to seem not a gate but a barrier. Yet the sense of what France has to offer has built up silently in the last thirty or forty years until now, with my seventy-second birthday behind me, I am about to go and live in Provence. So much am I of the past that since I began to write I have always speculated on this likelihood, for after all, where do flies go in the winter time? Writing for me still recalls Katherine Mansfield and Lawrence and Hemingway and Durrell and Graham Greene. 'You taught me everything a boy should know. Oh Paris! stay the same.' Thank you Maurice Chevalier.

But France is so much part of necessary life for me that I make no apology for there being no article on France in this collection.

Certainly very rapidly in the post-war years I began to add the rest of Europe to it. Germany to begin with, when my books (the post-Hitler mood? the publishing magic of Insel Verlag?) knew a surprising flourish – especially in Berlin. In that strange, intangible city, I walked, enchanted but always ready for a downput. Berlin charm came back to me later in Tokyo where courtesy had so illusive and fragile a nature. For instance in Berlin, at a large gathering of mainly University students, a young man rose with a delightful boyish smile. 'If you are a famous writer, why do you look like an old red-faced farmer?' he asked, and he matched his question by the conversion of his friendly shy smile into an aggressive contemptuous look. The young audience, girls and boys alike, followed his change of mood in their expression. Luckily, I was well cared for by my German publisher who was caring and charming alike, in Germany, England, and years later in Cyprus. In the last, I spent a few weeks in a flat owned by English residents (a Raj-like couple – the wife claiming to have been the

Near-Eastern counterpart of Vera Lynn). Depressed as I have found that I always become by an island's limitations, combined for me with an even greater depression – Greek food – when we met my former German publisher in the streets of Kyrenia it was a pleasant break. We took him, I remember, to a Persian hill ruin overlooking the Mediterranean. It was the sort of situation that, coming on top of depression, might have led me to suicide, but he was so happy with everything, that I was distracted. But on our return to Kyrenia, we immediately cancelled the rest of our stay in the flat and returned to England via Rome, where, as always, everything, architecture, painting, food, social life, cats fed by old ladies in the Forum, was so delightful that we both cheered up. Italy was a great revelation and excitement. It was here that I learned to combine travel with being a writer. The garden of my cottage in Suffolk is very super-looking for three-quarters of the year, but England in winter can only be enjoyed if you have a strong streak of that English plucky, fun-loving acceptance of discomfort. I don't have that. When I became a full-time writer I had to write much of the time indoors which I never really like, and found always very claustrophobic. All the same, plucky writing in galoshes, woollen scarves, overcoats, thermal underwear, I always hated and have always tried to avoid. Travelling to warmer places in the winter has been wonderful although financially ruinous, but it has been enjoyable and profitable.

It meant, however, taking travel for granted, only so could a change of place and language and diet be just a part of daily living. I have stayed in a very large number of Italian towns, I think that is why I have a much stronger sense of Italy than individual places. Of course, there are wonders that bring to my mind and my feelings Florence or Venice, or Naples or Turin, but what they awaken in me is eventually not their difference, but more strongly their likeness to one another. Only a few Italian cities like Milan shut their gates in my face. But that gives me a sense of selection that makes foreign places more real, more personal. Indeed it has always been my sense that a foreign country comes alive more fully if we select the places to stay as part of the grand force of driving about rather than stopping at any particular pre-selected place. What, of course, made abroad part of my life was the monstrous loss of Tony's job, an extreme of genteelly English puritanism, that to his great credit, I think, he has never allowed to alienate him from England itself. It was partly by enforced foreign travel that we built up our method of travelling: it depended upon a car, and Tony's driving, and experimentation between hotels and rented apartments. The avoidance of groups, packages and the seaside, has brought upon us endless charges of snobbery and extravagance, but the lure of expert lectures and instant holiday friends at very reasonable rates was not sufficient, and we have remained ignorant at great expense, not without making many friends, however.

Of course, a good invitation helps enormously, but there are many hazards. I have known them all in Poland, Czechoslovakia, and Soviet Russia itself. But you can't be sure of avoiding these even outside the Iron Curtain. When I was invited to the Adelaide Festival, a fellow guest was Yevtushenko, the Russian poet, whom I had already met in Leningrad. He was an exceptionally lively and charming young man. At the opening session of the Congress I made the opening speech in which I chose to dwell on the dangers to writers of State interference with what they wrote or said. I purposely, in order to make it easier for Yevtushenko, included Soviet Russia simply as part of this general charge, saying, perhaps a little unfairly, that I felt sure that he would agree with the general charge against regimes that behaved in this way. He brushed it to one side as a mistaken judgement. Now, early in the morning, about one or two a.m., he chose to get a Russian-speaking Australian girl to tell me that he absolutely agreed with what I had said, but could not say so in public. I might perhaps have let it pass, had he not insisted on saying a number of times that he loved so much to see me because I reminded him of his Father. He hoped, the interpreter said, that I should forgive him for not

7

having spoken out publicly, and would I show my friendship by joining him in a glass of champagne. I said, roughly, I remember, 'No, I damn well can't. Why does Yev think it worth his while to wake me up with all this rubbish. Take him and the champagne away.' It was not kind, or understanding, but I don't regret it.

Most writers give a pretty fair picture of their country's imperfections. As I have said in this collection the defect of travel in Japan lies in the degree to which the great Japanese courtesy and charm too often break down. I am reminded of my friend, the remarkable novelist, Yukio Mishima. For all his strange ways, he was a person of magnetic charm, quite separate from his very Japanese manner, as I know by the great appeal he made to people abroad. But it was not always so in his own country. On my last visit to Tokyo he gave a banquet of fine splendour for me – dishes flown up from the far South and flown down from the far North – hostesses of exceptional beauty and careful *naïveté* – but all threatened throughout by his own mood – this was the first inkling that I had of what was to be his tragic and horrible end. It seems that some remark of the English Ambassador about Japan's insufficient concern for the happiness of dogs had enraged Yukio. He ordered me to go to the Ambassador and extract an apology. I had a heavy programme and a short visit, and said I could not do what he asked. In the end Yukio said abruptly, to one of his friends, 'Get Angus Wilson prostitute.' Then he turned on leaving the room, and added, 'A very cheap one.' His mood, let me say at once, was full of rage, not of laughter. It was unpleasant and I was sad to lose a friend.

All my travels have been packed with interest, pleasure, and rich feeding of my appetites – aesthetic, intellectual, humorous, and human. As I have said the happiest were those in which I began to travel with Tony at our own will and speed. It happened first in Sicily, then in Morocco, then gradually almost all over the world, save for Central Africa and for Latin America. This last, most strangely, because the Amazon had

8

been so important for my imagination as a child. Central Portugal was to prove the most beguiling. From the sixties onwards I lectured and later taught in universities in the United States. There are only two very short pieces about America in this collection. Considering the impact people and places all over the States have made on me I don't know why I didn't try to write more. My experience of America has, fortuitously, been almost entirely nearly everywhere in the States apart from New York. New Yorkers, like Londoners, can afford to avoid thinking about the rest of their country. I dined with very wealthy people in Gramercy Park, where every other room was an elegant seventeenth- or eighteenth-century import from England; my hostess was a fine, beautifully-dressed woman in black velvet and diamonds. She charmingly got me to talk of my travels. I had not got far: from Australia to Egypt, and then on to Angkor Wat, I was, in fact, moving on to mention Trinidad, when she said, not crossly, nor mockingly, but very simply, 'Sounds provincial, to me.' Up to that point, I hadn't said a word about how much I had enjoyed travelling in the States. No doubt she would have thought that provincial too. Sadly, I don't know New York and, therefore, cannot share her view, but, if you like travelling, nowhere is provincial.

Angus Wilson

Some Japanese
Observations
1957

In 1957, along with Stephen Spender and others, I was an English delegate to the International Congress held in Japan by PEN (Poets, Essayists and Novelists). It was my first visit to Japan. I was very lucky to have been no nearer to the Japanese War than intelligence work, and I have tried in this article and the one that follows to be an impartial observer, to distance myself from Japanese militarism, the atrocities, and the impact and significance of Hiroshima and Nagasaki.

*

* *

*

I too was told that the Japanese do not understand the concepts of 'privacy' or of 'guilt'. My informants were not the same as those of Stephen Spender so that it seems likely this is one of the general ideas the Japanese have about themselves. (It is notable, by the way, that though they are constantly asking foreigners 'What do you think of us?' the replies do not seem greatly to affect the fixed body of *idées reçues* they already have about 'Japanese character, temperament,' etc.). I am unconvinced that the Japanese do not hold strict ideas of privacy and do not suffer great pangs of guilt. The difference between them and us in this is more, I think, one of kind. On occasion, when I felt peculiarly at home with Japanese people (and as the visit, short though it was, progressed, this was most of the time), I brought out a number of 'personal' statements about myself. The reaction was not wholly favourable. The older Japanese attempted, not very successfully, to overlook what they felt to be an odd breach of manners. The middle-aged and young (most of whom are anti-traditional and Westernizing-liberal, at any rate in aim if not in achievement), after a gulp, welcomed my indiscretions as a further blow to tradition. Both parties reported me as 'a man who forces us to change our view of what an English gentleman is like.' This verdict expressed by the older people was sharp and disapproving, the same verdict expressed by the younger group was admiring. Their surprise was doubled by the fact that I was English and the English are known for their reserve, but I saw nothing to confirm that the Japanese are any less reserved about their 'private affairs', although custom, of course, lays different emphasis on what is private and what not.

As to sense of sin or guilt, religion is far more broken down and for longer in Japan than with us, and sin in the sense we understand it is not an acutely-felt reality. But anxiety about breach of custom, of decorum, is still very strong: it is felt perhaps more strongly by those who would like to be free from it than sin is by non-Christians in Europe. Since this custom and decorum extends into every province of life I cannot believe that the burden of conscience for the Japanese is any less than for us. In fact, I suspect it is greater.

I doubt if the Japanese felt free to comment on some American authors' apparent drunkenness because they had no conception of private matters. (In any case, is drunkenness at a public reception by reporters a private matter?) They mentioned it because drunkenness alone, of the few boltholes that they have against the awful pressure of decorous and suitable behaviour, is regarded as a privileged, almost whimsical, behaviour. A drunken man is a privileged man, a sort of holy innocent. Many of the large number of drunks we saw in Japan were far less drunk than they pretended, but they were seizing the excuse to break through the barrier of social custom. A barrier that demands such means of evasion cannot, I believe, weigh much less heavily than our sense of sin, however different its origin.

I would note, by the way, that those drunks or pretended drunks to whom I talked behaved in fact only a very little differently from the others – they were the same polite, charming, and easily lovable people that one met most of the time. I cannot help suspecting that, though the circumscription of life presses irksomely upon many Japanese, especially upon younger ones, they do not have much idea or imagination of what they would or could do outside the confines of life as they know it. This may well relate to the overwhelming sense of

14

geographical isolation that one gets in Japan. A point to which I shall return.

*

All this brings me on to what has most preoccupied me in retrospect since I left Japan. What gave me such a very favourable impression of the Japanese people? I cannot easily find specific reasons for this general impression. A cynic might say that what delighted me in Japan was the fuss made of me. Anyone who saw me then would know that I enjoyed it. But lionizing, like *Gemütlichkeit* or charm, if they are backed up by no more than the desire to please, will pall after a very short while. Indeed the visitor is liable to feel he has been made a fool of and to react unfavourably in the end. It is a reaction one easily gets with, say, Austrians. That does not happen in Japan.

Again, many visitors to the PEN Congress pointed to the high position occupied by literature in Japan – the esteem enjoyed by authors in popular papers. They delighted in pointing out how what our International President called *'le petit peuple japonais'* treated writers as celebrities – they usually meant, of course, the chambermaids, restaurant hostesses, and barboys who had seen the photographs in the morning paper. In so far as this is not just a disguised way of saying that you like being lionized, it belongs to the familiar argument that artists are not sufficiently regarded in popular esteem by the English as they are in Europe. I have never myself felt that this sort of culture snobbery was either attractive in a nation or helpful to its literature. At its best, as in Scandinavia, where it really does mean more than snobbery and is in fact a general serious regard for the arts, it is, of course, commendable. It does not, however, necessarily make Scandinavians lovable. I doubt if the Japanese are as serious as the Scandinavians in their widespread profession of regard for culture, but they leave one with this curious feeling of affection for them.

Stephen Spender says that they are really interested in one's replies to their questions about Japan. They may be, but, as I have said, I doubt if they alter their stereotypes much as a result. He also said that they do not want polite answers. I'm not quite sure about this. I think they want interesting answers, and they probably feel that criticism is more interesting and, therefore, a greater praise than overt praise. But it is true a very high percentage of the middle-aged and younger people one meets are 'bothered and bewildered'. They are still reeling – as who would not be? – under Hiroshima. I did not find any growth yet of a 'younger still' body of opinion which was anxious to put, not only the failure of the old nationalism, but also the liberalizing, Westernizing reaction to it, behind them. When, if ever, this attitude appears it will be then that the present Weimarism may change into some new totalitarian movement. But I think Stephen Spender is right to point out that such Western historical analogies should not be too closely pressed upon Asian situations. Too many European or American commentators on the scene take it for granted that the present bewilderment and anxiety to achieve a Western liberal outlook among the younger Japanese will inevitably meet disillusion and cause a return to the voice of national demagogy. I even felt on occasion that for some Westerners the charm of the Japanese lay in their being a 'fated', or a 'lost people'.

This view, of course, fits in well with certain aspects of Japanese culture. Their literature, except for the odd novel like Ooka's *Fires on the Plain*, is permeated by this depressing and sterile nostalgia, this constant harping upon the fleetingness of beauty, of happiness, and of human life. For the older generation it still finds its expression – as we see in Kawabata's or Tanizaki's novels – in the old 'meeting and parting' ill-fated love affairs of Japanese traditional love and the traditional settings of the hot springs, the Noh and Kabuki plays, the geishas, the ceremonies of flower arrangement and tea-making, the contemplation of the autumn maple leaves changing colour. The fact that all this tradition is under fierce attack from the younger generation, and is possibly on the way out, only makes it seem to them a more fit – because more sad – subject for art. I find this aspect of Japanese culture highly depressing. It is tied to a dead Western world – to Maupassant, Chekhov, and most significantly Herman Hesse who is a living name to old and young alike. The tea-making and the flower decoration seemed to me arty and 'tatty' and I suspect that even the best art produced under the spell of all this shares in these unfortunate qualities. When we turn to younger generations we find that the same quality is there, though it seeks its inspiration in other Western models – Faulkner, Sartre, James Deanism, the Left Bank world. All these are loved mainly for their quality of sweet, autumn hopelessness. The name of Eliot's *Waste Land* – just the two words, not the poem – seems sometimes to hang like an evil and absurd charm over all this aspect of Japanese life.

Nevertheless, there is no doubt that part of the Japanese charm *does* lie in their mixed-up-kiddism. It has all the self-centredness of its Western counterpart, but it has got something more. Few Western mixed-up kids really want to solve their mix-up, even fewer have any energy or capacity to carry out any solution they are offered. But even the most coffee-bar Japanese are only so for certain hours of the day, and for very limited hours at that. For the rest of the time they follow a very different rôle – that of the Good Apprentice. They work, and work very hard. For an Englishman like myself – part romantic, part Calvinist – this makes them a very attractive people. The Good Apprentice and the mixed-up kid – it is not perhaps a very promising schizophrenia – one is taken back immediately to our old parallel of Weimar Germany. If the Good Apprentice was concerned only with self-satisfied self-advancement, it would not be very promising. There is a good deal of smug ambition, rugged individualism in the country which so welcomed Samuel Smiles when Western thought first came there. Personal ambition was even given to me as a reason for Japanese war atrocities – if atrocity was the means to promotion then let us excel in it in all ranks! It is a

17

very likely answer, I think. But there is not just self-seeking and dreaming of ideals, with no bridge between. I talked to more than one young man about the difficulties of improving economic conditions and strengthening trade unionism in a still paternalistic industrial framework, and their discussions were neither starry-eyed nor narrowly self-interested. If the mixed-up kids were all self-centredly taking pleasure in being mixed up, this would be as hopeless as it is in the West. But they do not like being mixed up, they are bored with it and actually – which is unusual for Japanese – laugh at it.

Or perhaps I am only saying that they are nearer to earth, as we understand it, more empirical than other Asians. For, of course, the Japanese gained greatly by being in the setting of a mixed congress of Westerners and Asians. They have, as I have written, their guilts and tensions in plenty, they have (the younger generation particularly) grave doubts of themselves; but they do not have that eroding inferiority complex which seeks to right itself in a constant stressing of moral and spiritual superiority over the West that is annoying among the bulk of, for example, Indians and Pakistanis and prevents them from making a contribution to discussions commensurate with their world importance. Nor do we ex-imperial nations of the West have the same inhibiting sense of guilt towards Japan that we have towards Indians or Pakistanis. Most Western delegates tried, and I am sure they were right, to throw off this sense of guilt, to admit the past and then to stress the useful contributions that the West can make to the East. But it is an uphill and perhaps hopeless task, at any rate for some decades. If we spoke of the value that differences between East and West meant for cultural reciprocity, we were interpreted as stressing the inferiority of the East. If, as Moravia did, we attempted an analysis of the benefit that humanism had made to civilization we were reminded of the failures of Western materialism, the deep untouched spiritual values of the East.

At times I felt that imperialism's guilt lay in exactly this – the rapid, high-minded generalizing mist into which Indian and

Pakistani thought had evaporated. To them our empiricism as well as our humanistic irony were only another repeat performance of shallow Western materialism. The Japanese – typical irony of history – got the praises of both sides. The West were in full sympathy with the younger generation, its doubts and determination, a little sceptical of the ivory tower of the older traditionalist Japanese writers. The Asians stress how much at home they felt in traditional Japan, pouring cold water on the younger Japanese, asserting that their Westernism and their doubts were a passing mood of youth. And, of course, how pleasant for us all to feel able so much to like hosts who had received us so warmly and with such charm.

*

Nevertheless I had more and more during my few weeks in Japan the feeling that these many hundred people to whom I spoke were, in their courageous efforts to realize themselves, living under a peculiar tension. Most people in most countries, of course, are living under tension – tensions peculiar to their countries, too, that go beyond global atomic threats, tensions of a nation on the way up or on the way down, or in the saddle and frightened of its position. The Japanese tension, I think, is peculiarly frightening because for many reasons it has reached the hypnotic stage. The stress of strenuous, solemn, comparatively unenjoyed play and of long, immolating hours of work threatens to be overwhelming – and however one may support the younger generation in their rejection of the old traditional life with its Samurai undertones, it did – I imagine, for the educated classes at any rate – provide a conscious relaxation which life in Japan sorely needs. As it is, I think, they are very near to exhaustion. Stephen Spender has said that unlike other Asian nations they have a standard of living, they know what it means, and they want to improve it. But nevertheless for millions of workers – blackcoated, intellectual, and manual – it is pitiably low. Moravia and I noticed how often in trains at midday and in cool weather, the occupants one and all fell

19

asleep. Tension that ends in lethargy could so well get into the debilitating, self-pitying, falling-leaf side of their cultural heritage and leave them open to the wiles of the first false siren song that reached their ears. And all this in the most claustrophobic isolation.

The isolation of most of the educated – and education, or at any rate literacy, is widespread – can hardly be conceived. Of, for example, all the vast number in this overcrowded island who know the English language well and its literature a little more hazily. When, unless they get the few rare grants or are successful businessmen, are they ever likely to go outside Japan? Academic knowledge of the English language is profound, so that a special pure English may well be found in Japan in a hundred years' time that is lost here or in the United States. But this is not the food they desperately seek. They are confined to their ugly cities – cities so threatened and so often demolished are necessarily so. They must make the most of Kyoto and Nara, which apart from the wonderful sculptures in the museums will hardly compare with the beauties of Western show-place cities or, for example, with Bangkok. True, of course, they have a picturesque countryside – part Switzerland, part Côte d'Azure, and on the coast at any rate wonderful and unique. But countryside is never the food for a restless, searching generation. Perhaps this accounts for two odd phenomena: for the totally neglected roads, creating a land of crowded train travel for the many and easy air travel for the business few – a land without the solace of motor-touring so essential to relieve the claustrophia of the middle classes in industrial countries; and for the strange fact reported to us, that there are large stretches of quite virgin land in the North despite the appallingly overcrowded towns of the centre.

I fear that I have allowed an excessive gloom to cover a land and people that I immensely liked. The truth is that all this is more potential than actual. The Japanese seldom smile, except to please Westerners, yet they do laugh and their laughter is not hysteric but is the result of a real sense of comedy and absurdity, a laugh of enjoyment. It is this that makes one ready to stand by one's conviction, so difficult to back up with examples, that the Japanese are not only moving and courageous, objects of compassion, but also intelligent and successful, subjects for admiration.

Night and Day
in Tokyo
1957

The first view of Tokyo as you leave the airport is hideous; so it is with most airports; unfortunately in this case the impression is a true foretaste. Tokyo is a very ugly city. It comprises, I was told, a slightly bigger area than Greater London and has a larger population. It depressed me very often to think of so many agreeable people – for the Japanese, despite many vices and weaknesses, are among the most *agreeable* people I have ever met – living in such ugly, drab surroundings.

A great deal of the city, of course, was still being rebuilt, and building operations seemed always to demand a profusion of concrete blocks, sand or cement heaps, wooden frames and other paraphernalia extending far beyond the immediate building sites. The new Tokyo promises to be impressive rather than beautiful. Earthquakes prevent the construction of skyscrapers, and the height of buildings is regulated by law. But with that somewhat shallow interpretation of 'modern' which reigns in some, though not all, Japanese circles, 'biggest and best' is the order of the day.

The new buildings in the Marumouchi business and official area and along the Ginza, Tokyo's West End, have that look of modern architecture which has not quite dared to go the whole hog – a look familiar enough, God help us, in London, also a city of skyscraper-prohibition, but worse in Tokyo because the architects have made up what they are not allowed in height by odd and extravagant 'modern' details.

All this side of Tokyo, symbolized by the neon-lighted Ginza at night with its crowds of awe-struck, gaping country and provincial visitors, is ostentatious and garish. In the outer wards, it is true, I saw a number of new housing estates, schools and office buildings in a conventional modern glass and concrete idiom that was up to the best European standard. Some visitors were busy lamenting the fact that the new housing of multiple-storey flats will replace the old single-storeyed wooden houses; but for anything that I saw, except for farmhouses in the country and occasional rich men's houses, the sooner the old traditional Japanese house goes, the better, so far as external appearance is concerned.

Perhaps I have been more critical of Tokyo's appearance than is fair, but, at the back of my mind, was always the feeling that Tokyo, city of natural disasters, was the model of the future cities of the world in an atomic age – a mixture of improvized shoddiness and eternal rebuilding. Certainly the outsides of Tokyo houses give no clue to the beauty within. In the same way, the streets of Tokyo and, in particular, the traffic, are no clue to the Japanese people. I have never seen or heard a noisier, more apparently disorganized stream of traffic. A taxi ride is far more alarming than in Paris, surpassed, I am told, only by Mexico City: pedestrians swarm across, jay-walk, hop, jump and shout; the pavements are forever giving out where building is in progress; trolley buses swerve in and out alarmingly; bicycles abound; the Vespa, Lambretta invasion is not so complete yet as in Germany or Italy, but if anything, noisier. It is as though a film set of city life had been specially prepared to be stared at by country hicks; and gape indeed they do – the vast army of peasant sightseers, and vendors of country produce, and unemployed from an over-populated, over-cultivated countryside.

*

Perhaps it is not true to say that all this gives no clue to the Japanese. If the hustle and noise and the jumbled flashy and

26

drab exteriors are taken to suggest that Tokyo people are 'tough' or confident or high-spirited, it might perhaps please some of them, but it would, I am sure, be a wrong interpretation. But if it is taken to suggest a people living on their nerves, deeply divided within themselves, it comes very near to the truth.

I am reminded here once again of my arrival in Tokyo. We travelled to the famous Imperial Hotel in a coach with a young Japanese girl as a guide. I already realized from the reporters that among the younger generation at any rate the English I should meet would be American English. But they had learned their American, as had the hundreds of students, young businessmen, bar hostesses, intellectuals and so on that I met later, either in the States or from reputable teachers at school or in the University. Our coach guide had picked hers up and with it the ideas of a sophisticated, attractive Western girl. What she said was largely unintelligible and her manner was a travesty of 'peppiness' that reminded me of a film star of my youth – Clara Bow, the It girl. It was a pathetic and dated performance.

Unfortunately the other travellers, being French, understood less of it than I did, and being tired and French they made no attempt to conceal their dislike of the high, harsh noise of our guide's voice coming through the loudspeaker. For some time she did not realize the effect she had produced, but when she did, all the jauntiness went out of her usherette's pillbox hat and uniform. We only just got to Frank Lloyd Wright's Imperial Hotel in time. A second later she would have lost all face in every sense by bursting into tears. She had wanted so much to please.

I was soon to realize how much every Tokyo citizen wishes to please. Of course, a great deal of this is the natural politeness of a very polite race. For example, the elderly lady – famous dramatist and poet – who, immediately on meeting me, asked if I was constipated by the Toyko air, was joining natural courtesy with a mistaken idea of 'emancipated conversation'. I, too, wanted to please, and made similar mistakes – it's

27

impossible not to do so in a country where custom and precedent are so different; but my Japanese hosts took infinite pains to prevent me seeing my mistakes; they thought I would mind not pleasing as much as they do – to the point, perhaps, of tears which come easily to them.

*

This, feverish, unbalanced side of Tokyo comes out, as one would expect, most strongly in the night life. The Japanese work feverishly to catch up again with the West, and they also seem to feel that they should play as feverishly, or even more so. True enough Tokyo night life is largely over before midnight, but while it is on it is an all out, exhausting affair; exhausting but very pleasant. It is partly so successful *because* they try so hard. They are naturally, I think, sad, sentimental, cruel, gentle – mixed-up kids, in fact, as some of the younger Tokyo generation will soon tell you – yet not naturally high-spirited. Nevertheless, they are desperate to know how to 'have a good time' and to give the visitor one; and, on the whole, they succeed. Also no Tokyo person can fail to decorate the interior of any room with grace and beauty, and to perform any act of service with dignity and charm.

The night clubs and bars, entirely Western though they are in inspiration, are never depressing or squalid; the waitresses, hostesses and barboys never rude or offhand. The motive, of course, as anywhere else is commercial, but I truly believe that in Tokyo it is forgotten for a large part of the time. Almost every Tokyo ward has its own pleasure quarter, as it has its own shopping centre, big department store and parks. The area around the Ginza, of course, is a West End, or rather a Montmartre.

The Shinzuku area is the Montparnasse, newest, most popular, patronized by students, intellectuals, young workers (both manual and white-collar). Even with a party of foreigners, but more particularly if I was with Japanese people, the evening always went well because everyone tried hard and successfully. Even so, the large number of drunks, and even more those who tried to appear more drunk than they were, showed how desperate was the attempt to break through the natural shell of convention and reserve.

The tourist cabaret night-clubs, like the 'Queen Bee' and the 'Papagayo', are imitation Western, but something which is quite their own, as individual as Japanese crooners and Japanese 'pop' numbers, or the Japanese Teddy Boys in the 'Tennessee' coffee bar. The best example, however, of the extraordinary Japanese adaptation of Western amusements is Pachinko.

On any night, in the main streets of Tokyo, you may see through brightly-lit windows of five- or six-storeyed modern buildings rows upon rows of men apparently performing some ritual – demanding automatic and rhythmic movement of the arms. These men are, in fact, playing pinball, called Pachinko. One can only imagine that, after hours of automatic work in factories, they are unable to leave off their routine movements. More rewarding, one would think, would be the boxing matches held out in the Ryoguku Stadium on the Sumida river.

Although the profusion of trick neon lighting advertisements is perhaps a bit vulgar, there is no doubt that simple words, probably, in fact, only the equivalent of Oxo or Jeyes Fluid, do look very beautiful to a foreign eye when flashed through the darkness in Japanese characters. Even more attractive are the lantern-lit narrow streets of huddled houses behind the main thoroughfares. Many of these belong to the Old Akasen red-light district. Defeat in war seems to have a rather peculiar effect upon the 'pleasure life' of a nation, and, as in Berlin of the nineteen-twenties, there are many rather strange 'private shows' at which the unsuspecting inquisitive visitor may find himself. I write 'are', though it should perhaps be 'were', for I understand that these shows have been cleaned up in the last months, although the red-light districts, formally closed down, have reappeared rather charmingly as Shiro Sen or White Light districts – a naïve idea of reform. All this night life, however, is for tourists, a small number of habitués, and Tokyo citizens on the occasional spree. Social life for all classes of people, and not only for the younger generation, increasingly revolves around coffee bars. They were a great pleasure to me, because in them I could forget Japanese food.

*

Japanese food was always a great 'problem' for me. I love food, and I pride myself on easy adaptation to foreign tastes, but Japanese meals are more to be seen than to be eaten. The best restaurants in the Sukiji or the Akasaka areas are very expensive, and there is no doubt that you get the full works for your money. The settings are enchanting: in the most elegant Japanese houses with sliding panels of varied coloured woods, screens letting in shafts of light, beautiful porcelain dishes, vistas of strange little gardens of rocks and pools and dwarf trees, flower decorations that are simple but breathtaking.

The hostesses at such restaurants, who sit beside you, filling your glass with sake as soon as it is emptied, are beautiful girls in colourful and elegant kimonos; they are less exotic than the professional geishas, but the geishas never looked quite human to me. The food comes in course after course, charmingly arrayed in tasteful colours, deliciously scented – but, to my mind, almost inedible. The sukiyaki meals, with the stringy steak soaked in egg yolk, I found nauseating; the tempura, as long as one did not touch the sauce which is their speciality, just all right. So many of the delicacies – grinko roots and lotus roots – have no taste at all. At the end of the meal, apart from rice and soup of which there is an endless quantity, you have only a sense of emptiness. I preferred always the cheap eel restaurants. There is, however, an excellent expensive French restaurant – The France-Za; and the Grill Room at The Imperial is a passable grill. I lunched once at a banquet of Japanese industrialists. The food was European, very sparse, and of boarding-house standard; light beer or fruit juice to drink. Looking at the rows and rows of enormously fat, babyfaced, ruthless-eyed businessmen, I compared them with their expense-sheet opposite numbers in England, and wondered if their lunch-time moderation did not account for much Japanese commercial success.

After the grander Japanese meal, however, is the time for the best of all Japanese institutions – the bath. The baths in the pleasure districts – Tokyo Onsen in Ginza, and Santhe in Shinjuku – are perhaps the most convenient for visitors; but every district has its public baths. To me the Tokyo bath ritual with its soaping – it is a deadly sin to let any soap get into the bath itself – its back-scrubbing girls and its increasingly hot sulphur pools, was the most pleasurable aspect of a city with a very humid climate in summer and autumn. The larger baths, with their cavernous grottoes, steamy smoke and figures lolling in and out of the pools, seem like a bank holiday in Inferno and have all the relief that such a day would give to the damned. After the baths, the next most pleasing Tokyo features are the parks and gardens – moss gardens, rock gardens, and enchanting dwarf gardens. The large Ueno Park (with Zoo) and Hibuja Park are both beautiful, but I think I should choose the Shinjuku Gardens as the most delightful of all.

*

Finally, a word about the most exotic feature – the Japanese theatre. Noh, the earliest type of play, with its strange ritual dances and primitive music, is seen in Tokyo now, I believe, only on special occasions. The Kabukiza theatre, a magnificent auditorium and a large Lyceum-theatre-type revolving stage, shows regularly programmes that last for hours. These highly stylized melodramas, dating from the eighteenth century, with their female parts played by men, can get a bit tedious, but the scenery is magnificent and the periodic, guttural cries of the audience calling for their favourite actors from the darkness has a strange, eerie effect. The puppet plays, tediously long, if impressive as shows of manual dexterity, are confined to Osaka. All this traditional theatre of Tokyo is steeped in the feudal ideas of the past – unquestioning service to the lord, military bravery, suicide. They are anathema to the younger generation, who genuinely seek to get away from the ideas that led Japan to disaster in the 'thirties and 'forties. I was moved to tears by the beauty of the Noh play that I saw. But when I rushed to give my impressions to a very intelligent, sympathetic young woman journalist, I was, for the only time in Japan, rather brusquely treated. 'All right!' she said. 'You loved it, although you didn't understand a word.'

Alas! There was no later. And when I think of returning to Tokyo, which I often do, it is not so much the city, fascinating and sometimes beautiful though many things are, that I look forward to seeing again, as the friends I made, especially the younger generation, Westernizing, often comic in their admiration for Sartre or James Dean, yet fighting a desperate battle for a good life in a country, terrifyingly isolated, over-populated, undernourished and traditionally sad. With all their hopes, they have the natural Japanese pessimism about their chances. I wish I could think they were wrong.

The Jolliest Resort
in the World
1958

Brighton is seen at its best from the sea. Most European seaside resorts – even those of the Mediterranean – are designed by the flashy bad taste of their architecture to fix the visitor's gaze seaward. Brighton, like Britannia, sets out to rule the waves and succeeds.

The prospect from a fishing smack or a yacht is enchanting. At this proper distance the Regency squares and terraces reveal their pleasing ordered symmetry; the Oriental absurdity of King George IV's Royal Pavilion seems no longer a gimcrack touring-company set for *Ali Baba and the Forty Thieves*, but the extravagant essence of the *Arabian Nights*; the few mid-Victorian monster hotels which mar the Regency regularity of the sea front seem only the odd, delightful extravagances which we expect and welcome in the truly well-bred; the hinterland of the large town, whose streets share the muddled ugliness which nineteenth-century free enterprise stamped on most English provincial towns, now rolls away in vague splendour to blend with the green hills of the South Downs behind.

You can almost get the right impression from the end of Brighton's two great piers, but to do the thing properly you should take all the risks of being afloat. I exaggerate these risks, perhaps, for I have never learned to swim. I owe the resort a grudge for this, since it was in the Brighton swimming baths that, as a small boy, suspended on a pair of bright pink rubber wings, I first completely failed to learn this useful art. Yet, all grudges forgotten, any day I would gladly take the risk of drowning in order to get this superb view.

*

Unfortunately, the visitor to Brighton seldom gets his first impression from the sea. Brighton is normally approached by road or railway and neither prospect entirely pleases. The motorist fares better than the traveller by train. The Sussex countryside – first the remains of a great forest, the medieval home of outlaws, and then the rolling Downs – used to be one of England's beauty spots. It remains attractive, but subtly suburbanized in the way that all Sunday-afternoon motoring country inevitably becomes – a faint flavour of Old World tearooms and the sudden voices of picnickers the other side of the bush pervades even its more remote and beautiful corners.

The road that leads from Brighton railway station to the sea front, on the other hand, has few compensations. English main railway termini nearly always accrue a huddle of hideous shops and lodging houses which recall the more squalid and petty sides of late Victorian crime; Brighton is not an exception to this English manner of welcoming visitors. There used at one time to be a shop window near Brighton station full of warnings of the Last Judgement and the Wrath to Come, which gave one a sort of macabre urge to hurry on. Modernization seems to have removed these admonitions which, in any case, are superfluous these days. On the whole, however, in summer-time – and to get the full flavour of Brighton you should visit it in summer – the railway is a better bet than the road. Holiday crowds in railway stations – and only crowd lovers should visit Brighton – have colour and life; the homebound motor-car crawl is the contemporary symbol of living death.

*

Superb architecture, tonic air and fascinating crowds are Brighton's three greatest attractions. On the front, which stretches for seven miles, the foreign visitor who has a fancy

36

to see something of all types of English life may do so on a fine summer day more comfortably and completely than anywhere else in England. He will not see all types, though, for Brighton, which one hundred and fifty years ago was the centre of aristocratic and fashionable life, is certainly no longer aristocratic and hardly fashionable; the fashionable and the aristocratic are, in any case, severely diminished in modern England. It is not, all the same, predominantly middle-class like Bournemouth or Torquay, nor predominantly working-class like Southend. In my youth I was frequently taken for holidays to 'unspoilt' seaside places like Brighton's neighbour, Seaford, because the common people did not go there. This experience more than any other has led me to love Brighton, which in my parents' eyes was the most 'spoilt' of all seaside resorts, except, perhaps, Southend, which, in any case, people of our class did not visit. Brighton is often called London-by-the-Sea, but the title says too much and too little. It is foolish to claim the richness and variety of London for any other English town, yet London's vastness tends to overcrowd the canvas, to merge and subdue even the sharp outlines of England's social order.

Brighton reflects enough of London's details and in its boisterous, buoyant air the details stand out with photographic sharpness. Country people in for shopping mingle their broad Sussex accent with the thick glottal Cockney of working-class families from London. A grand county lady, with that look of unease in walking that only the habitual fox hunters can acquire, passes the 'fast' retired Edwardian actress whose unease in walking comes from the days when beautiful women did not take exercise. The retired colonel's wife contrasts her socially superior dowdiness with the 'un-English' svelte smartness of a buyer for one of London's dress shops. The drainpipe narrowness of the London Teddy Boys' trousers agrees with the width of the old sporting baronets', if in everything else they are poles apart.

Mum and Dad eat whelks or cockles heavily soused in

vinegar, but the shadow of Americanization hangs over the kids' bright pink sticks of candy floss. Mum lifts up her skirts, and Dad rolls up his trousers, to paddle at the sea's edge; but their teenage children equal Cannes in their swimming trunks and bikinis. The teenagers, too, will rock-and-roll in the town's many dance halls, but Mum and Dad will listen to the band on the pier which still spells safety for England in 'Airs from Gilbert and Sullivan', 'Selections from *The Maid of the Mountains*', or, daringly, *Rose Marie*.

Many a middle-class father will note the whelks and cockles and the paddling with approval, feeling that the old British working class which he could patronize is not yet dead. All is well with England, he will feel, while huge sticks of pink-and-white candy are offered for sale, or the familiar post-cards with their fat ladies in bathing costumes or girls with their skirts caught in the breeze are on display. It is a sentimentalism that the respectable suburban gentleman shares all unknowingly with George Orwell, who once praised the post-cards in an essay. Orwell, no doubt, would have disapproved of the Teddy Boys and the accent on American film stars in the waxwork displays or the standardized show girls who have replaced the naughty Edwardian ladies with their frilly underwear in the 'What the Butler Saw' peep shows on the piers. But for the impartial visitor from abroad, untroubled by dreams of England's 'good old days', the Brighton summer scene is an excellent introduction to the society in transition which makes modern England so fascinating a study in human behaviour.

*

Brighton is no longer a holiday resort but one of England's largest residential towns. With its sister town of Hove it has a population of 228,000. Only a proportion of these are the tradesmen, hotel and lodging housekeepers or amusement mongers who entertain the visitors. There is a large resident population of retired people, though the sad, muted note which too often hangs around spas or seaside towns mainly given up to the retired, is absent. Here the elderly and the convalescent are swallowed up in the mass. Only occasionally when the winter sun is peculiarly bright does the sea front have that slow processional look common in towns like Bath or Harrogate, where old age is ostentatiously making the best of a little fine weather.

A large part of Brighton's population since mid-Victorian days has spent its working life in London – stockbrokers, lawyers and even clerks in their City clothes – suffering each summer morning as they pass the first rush of tourists at the station. Since Victorian times, too, there has been a large semi-resident population of middle-class boys and girls – pupils of the numerous private schools that cluster on the downland edges of the town. Prominent on the east side of Brighton, at the height of a great cliff overlooking the sea, is the too prominent structure of Roedean School – one of the best-known girls' private schools and symbol of England's hockey-playing womanhood. The boisterous east winds can no doubt be relied on to blow away from the broad playing fields the least vestige of what is not truly British.

All this resident population belongs to the solid middle class who traditionally return Tory members of Parliament for Hove and Brighton. Since the last war, however, industry has increased and a large engineering works is bringing working-class housing estates to the perimeter of the town. If, in addition, the project for setting up a 'red brick' university in Brighton matures, the once aristocratic, now middle-class, town may join the world of welfare England to the horror, no doubt, of landladies, stockbrokers, retired admirals, and private-school teachers alike. Perhaps then Brighton may be the first seaside town to desert from the traditional Toryism of English holiday resorts.

*

The growth of a Brighton that is divorced from the visitor has dimmed inevitably a little of the colourfulness of the town, particularly in the shopping streets and suburbs. Nevertheless, the sea front retains its traditional boisterous jollity; and the note of raffishness, of 'naughtiness', that has been associated with the name 'Brighton' ever since the days of the Regent and his 'wicked' friends, is still there.

To begin with, Brighton has special associations with the stage and the sporting world. In mid-Victorian times, when the new spirit of middle-class prudishness reacted strongly against the surviving pockets of Regency manners in Brighton, the outraged societies for moral reform pointed to the music halls as the focal points of vice. The old music hall hardly survives in England today.

Variety stars, however, still make their homes in Brighton, although it is significant that the top celebrity on the Brighton Publicity Department's list of notable residents is Mr Gilbert Harding, the TV and radio king of quiz masters. The legitimate-theatre managements, however, still regard Brighton audiences as a good test for pre-London try-outs; although the holiday mood of Brighton's Theatre Royal audiences is probably kinder it is no less sophisticated than that of the smart London first-nighters. Brighton remains, too, a great holiday place and residential centre for the stage world. The old Regency tradition of 'sport', defined as horse racing and boxing, has also survived. For one generation of Englishmen Brighton is symbolized by the late Harry Preston, proprietor of the Royal Albion Hotel, friend of the Duke of Windsor (then Prince of Wales) and of Arnold Bennett, Edgar Wallace and other sports-loving celebrities of the 1920s, and promoter of boxing matches at the Regent's Royal Pavilion.

Something of Brighton's sporting fame and perhaps the last touch of the Regency bucks died with Preston, but faithful to its tradition of 'being in the swing', Brighton has in its Tigers one of the foremost ice-hockey teams of England. Their matches are played in the Sports Stadium which stands on the site of the King's Head Inn, pulled down in the 1930s. It is perhaps a fitting site, for from this inn our most 'sporting' King Charles II made his escape in 1651 from the forces of Puritanism. On the Downs to the north-east stands the racecourse. The August meetings are famous, nor does their association with the tougher section of the racing world seem to diminish. My father, a racing man of the 1880s and 90s, used to speak of the Brighton meeting as the event of the racing year at which the 'boys' congregated to relieve the unwary or unprotected successful 'punter' of his winnings. I was reminded of this when I first read Graham Greene's *Brighton Rock* with its background of race gangs and Bookmakers' Protection Associations.

*

The Regency raffish note, revived by Edward VII when he was Prince of Wales, has stuck to Brighton in the English middle-class mind, despite its long establishment as a family holiday resort. Its nearness to London in both distance and sophistication makes it the most likely place for London crooks or roughs on the spree, but criminal statistics hardly bear out the lurid implications of *Brighton Rock*. The sensational murders, in fact, have tended to occur more in the respectable sister resort of Eastbourne.

The truth is that Brighton is large enough to include the disreputable among its great mass of respectability. Certainly suburban fathers still like to wink at the name of Brighton, to suggest that Paris does not stand alone as the rendezvous for 'naughty' weekends. This fable, however, like many another *naïveté*, including the idea of the naughty weekend itself, has almost disappeared even in darkest suburbia today. The old prurient leer is dying in England with the old prudish frown from which it was bred; a new Puritanism, it is true, has sprung up among the younger generation, but it is more sophisticated and has not yet revealed its prurient side.

The peep shows on the piers with their standardized cheesecake instead of the Edwardian frillies which survived until after the last war marked the beginning of the end; now only the post-cards with their jokes about landladies, policemen and fat ladies bathing remain to shock an occasional old-fashioned magistrate and delight an occasional old-fashioned commercial traveller on the spree.

The underworld, the illicit lovers, the stage, the sporting world, and the ordinary holidaymaker still have one common weakness, however, which Brighton reflects – a superstitious curiosity about their futures. Brighton abounds in fortune-tellers of all kinds – palmists, crystal-gazers, and mediums who since the end of the last century have administered to the hypochondriacs of the soul as the founders of Brighton's medical fame once administered to the hypochondriacs of the body.

One of my earliest memories of Brighton is of a proxy aunt, an Edwardian actress, who in her pursuit of the occult allowed her opals to be dematerialized by a Eurasian gentleman in return for a string of 'spirit' beads made somewhat oddly of wood. Today every crystal-gazer, chiromancer, and clair-voyant on the sea front and on the piers displays testimonials from stars of the stage and film world, from jockeys and other devotees of 'the fancy'. Something of the fashionable Victorian interest in the occult remains in the name of Dr Mesmer Berg, who claims to have brought belief in the unseen to heavyweight champions and to an Indian maharaja.

My own experience with the famous Madame Binnie, who holds court on the Palace Pier, was a little more obscure. She seemed, despite my white hairs, to connect me with the dancing profession and promised me success in my unrealized ambitions through partnership with a lady described as 'petite', by which Madame Binnie explained that she meant, indicating her bust, 'not large here'. She also reminded me that three weeks or, possibly, months before my interview with her, I had 'gone on the raz' to ease my despair at my failed dancing ambition. She advised me not to do this again in a kindly, matey tone and not in a spirit of moral censure. It was a cozy if unilluminating glimpse into the unseen.

The occult apart, however, the entertainments provided

in Brighton today are becoming standardized to the modern pattern. The Aquarium suggests something of the old 'improving' Victorian diversions, but even here the fish tanks have been brought up to date by the importation of Walt Disney-like stone dwarfs around whose whimsy the fishes swim with a disdainful, cynical look. Pierrots are still to be seen in summer, but television is unlikely to leave them a much longer life. Brighton, unlike Blackpool and Southend, has never boasted large amusement parks with big wheels. Side shows and shooting galleries on the piers still draw troops of youths, but I suspect the dance halls with rock-and-roll draw more.

*

If, however, Brighton seems to the middle-aged like myself to have lost something to standardization – and the more uniform society of modern England is perhaps seen at its worst in the entertainment it seeks and offers – it still retains enough character to outdo any other English seaside town in the pleasures it offers. To walk the King's Road, the sea promenade, and note the guests on the terraces and at the windows of the big hotels, still delights me as it did when I was a schoolboy. Quiet and rich at the Grand; more flamboyantly rich at the Metropole; colonels and bookmakers; chorus girls and clergymen's widows – against the wonderful background of Regency terraces and crescents it seems the embodiment of Thackeray's *Vanity Fair*. For, in the last resort, Brighton stands or falls by its background of history that reflects England's changes for the last two hundred years.

Brighton's history for the ordinary English visitor, however, is centred in its golden age – the Regency. The period lasted nine years, 1811–20, during which George, Prince of Wales (later George IV) acted for his father, George III. In the popular imagination it was an age of aristocratic eccentricity and naughtiness; even among the more serious and sophisticated middle classes of modern England the Sins of Society with two capital S's are still a great draw. The Regent himself has never been so popular a figure of historical romance as our other great amorous monarch, Charles II – not, I suspect, because he was more caddish, but because he was so grossly fat and went too far in aristocratic eccentricity by wearing corsets. The age of the Bucks, however, of the Dandies and of the Macaronis (fops) has been familiar to historical-novel readers since Conan Doyle's *Rodney Stone*, and Brighton has been the glamorous historic centre of their fabulous drinking, gambling and general hell-rakery.

More recently, however, Regency Brighton has had an added historical attraction for the middle-class visitors who never open more than a woman's magazine. It is ten years or more now since Regency taste dropped from the smart world down to suburbia, and there, judging by the furniture shops, it still holds sway, although seriously threatened by the 'contemporary'. As a result the Royal Pavilion, that strange, many-domed Oriental extravagance in which the Regent lived, draws a continuous stream of visitors. It was designed originally in the 'Hindustan Style', and was completed by John Nash in 1822. To the visitor who has already seen the terraces and squares of Brighton's front and has learned to call their symmetrical neatness 'Regency', the Pavilion must be hard indeed to fit in the pattern.

Most visitors, however, find it quite enchanting. The interior, too, must be something of a puzzle to the ladies from the suburbs who have furnished their rooms in 'Regency Style', for they will find little of those striped satin papers, gold-and-white-striped fabrics and blue ceilings with gold stars that represent Regency taste in a hundred country hotels or small clubs furnished in Regency taste since the war. The opulent and exotic rooms, under Mr Clifford Musgrave's curatorship, have been restored to their original furnishings and even the original wall paint is being recovered. The colours are hard greens and staring pinks, deep yellows and scarlets, the ceilings are magnificent with dragons and serpents, the organ in the music room is decorated beyond credulity. Faced

44

by this unashamed extravagance a good number of the visitors seem to take refuge in staring upward at the glass chandeliers. I have seen this retreat practised in every palace where splendour is too strong for modern taste – at Versailles, in the baroque palaces of Germany, in the rococo monasteries, above all at Mad Ludwig's in Bavaria. Visitors rivet their eyes on the chandeliers as though afraid they may fall from the ceiling.

The most popular room in the Pavilion seems to be the vast kitchen arranged with rows and rows of dummy joints of meat, of dummy game and fish as for a royal banquet. At the far end a spit turns continuously with a whole model ox. Once again the crowd seem to feel safe with this as they do with the giant clock at Beauvais Cathedral – at least something is moving. An unexpected piece of realism has crept into the Regent's kitchen, however, in the shape of a large stuffed rat. When I was there last, two pleasant middle-aged ladies were much upset by it. 'I'm sorry they should have that there,' said one, and the other, 'Yes, quite out of keeping.' They spoke as though they might have expected to find innumerable large rats in the kitchens of their own homes, but not in a royal palace; a nice respectful attitude, I felt. All in all, the Royal Pavilion is one of the great houses most worth seeing in England and as every month seems to add another to the list of mansions 'open to the public' it is as well to have some priority. Nevertheless, I could do without the subdued sound of Haydn and Mozart string quartets that follows one round the rooms; this recalls for me not the court of the Prince Regent but somewhat tedious evenings after dinner at some cultured English home in Hampstead. (Good music is surely meant to be listened to, not to make a background of period taste.)

The other historic part of Brighton which draws visitors is the little quarter of narrow streets called the Lanes. Apart from the Ship Hotel it is all that remains of Brighton before the Regent made it splendid. These winding alleyways are largely given over to antique shops, and visitors seem to love them, especially on wet days. Personally, I do not find browsing around junk shops a very satisfactory way of spending time. If there are things that I want, enough other people want them to make them beyond the reach of my purse; and what I can afford are as a rule objects for which I would not provide house room even if they were given to me. But for those who continue faithfully to believe that they have an eye for low-priced objects of beauty and antiquity the Lanes make an excellent hunting ground. And there are a number of 'ladies' tearooms' to provide them with coffee and oatcake when they grow tired. Ladies' tearooms, by the way, are an interesting survival from pre-Welfare State days, for the ladies referred to are the proprietresses. As to oatcakes, these are a sticky mixture of porridge oats and golden syrup, the main contribution made by ladies' tearooms to the English cuisine. Since the Lanes are a survival of Brighton in its pre-Regent days, I should be sorry to see them go.

*

Of all the periods of Brighton's history, which mirrors England's social history so exactly, the period from 1750 to 1790 seems to me the most extraordinary and the most delightful. What is so enchanting about these first forty years of Brighton's fashionable existence is their complete remoteness. Today the hydropathic theories of Dr Richard Russell and Dr Anthony Relhan, who in turn made Brighton the healing spring for the hypochondriacs of London's *beau monde*, seem almost like Groucho Marx in action.

No one before Doctor Russell had seriously considered sea water either for external or internal application. It had been supposed a cure for hydrophobia, but even in eighteenth-century England mad dogs were the exception rather than the rule. Fashionable folk soon flocked to the little village, for Doctor Russell suggested that sea bathing would cure many of the innumerable ills that the frowsty air, the over-drinking and over-eating eighteenth-century London brought upon its smarter residents. The sea bathing was not intended as in any way pleasurable and indeed it could not have been so. In 1782 the novelist Fanny Burney took her curative swims with Mrs Thrale, Samuel Johnson's friend, shortly before dawn in the month of November: it requires experience of the usual English November weather to realize the full horror of such an experience. Ladies and gentlemen, of course, bathed in separate parts of the beach. (The guidebooks contained sly jests about the gentlemen's telescopes for many decades.) Male and female attendants respectively waited upon the gentlemen and ladies at the bathing machines. Nobody, of course, looked at the sea. Lakes and mountains had already become 'sublime', but the beauties of nature did not yet encompass oceans.

In this early crazy season of Brighton's fashionable history the visitors were kept far too busy by the doctors' malicious tricks to have leisure for nature's parables. To Doctor Russell's winter swims at dawn his successor Doctor Relhan added the necessity of swallowing copious draughts of sea water. It only remained for his successor, Doctor Awister, to make the cure more palatable. 'To remove the loathing, sickness and thirst with which sea water, taken pure, is always attended,' he wrote, 'it should be mixed with an equal quantity of new milk. Thus it becomes a noble medicine.'

Much of this invalidish, crank world of the mid-eighteenth century was swept away by the arrival of the Regent's court at the end of the 1780s. The prince himself was still a good-looking, lively man and had no wish to be surrounded by the moribund, while the fashionable invalids, many of whom suffered from 'nerves' – a complaint almost as common then as now – found the roistering rakes a little too loud for their taste. However, crank Brighton lingered on with the chalybeate springs magniloquently called 'Stromboli' after the volcano, with Turkish baths known as shampoos and with the spa which provided imitations of all the German medicinal waters.

Mr Nathan Smith came there in 1799 with his air pump to extract the gout; and as late as 1811 we find Teddy Palmer, the local blacksmith, relieving the Regent's toothache by directing streams of hot smoke into his mouth. It must have been the last decrepit remnants of the wicked Regency – gentlemen in the last extremes of corseting and ladies with a prodigiously shocking amount of rouge – who still visited the springs or called for the 'warm sea water baths with hot linen sent to any part of the town on the shortest notice', which were still advertised in 1861. By that date the Court had long since left, the Pavilion was regarded as a monstrosity, the railway had brought the middle classes to Brighton and 'many thousands of London people, merchants, bankers, stockbrokers and the like make it their permanent home'. If any of the 'frail daughters of Venus' referred to in Regency guides still survived, their frailty must have been largely in memory; and they would surely have been past needing the asylum of the newly founded 'Brighton Home for Female Penitents' by which Victorian ladies hoped to reclaim this black spot of lingering eighteenth-century vice.

*

In Brighton, more than in any other English city, I think, the gradual growth of one way of living from another can be clearly seen. The Lanes must have been at once a source of curiosity and of incredible increase in revenue to the inhabitants of this isolated little place, so nearly threatened with extinction by sea floods only two decades before. After the Lanes, the Steine, the great open space used by these impoverished fishermen for drying their nets and now a pleasant modern town garden; but in the heyday of the Regent it was the centre of court life, with fishing nets banished, for though picturesque they no doubt smelt too strongly. Many of the fine aristocratic houses survive, though some, like poor Mrs Fitzherbert's house, where she bore the Regent's ill-treatment of her so stoically, is now refaced and spoiled. Then the great terraces and squares along the King's Road, which was made in 1822. From the 1830s onwards they appeared, and, indeed, when 'Regency' architecture had long given place to Victorian styles in other parts of England, as late as the 1860s, houses in this style were still being erected in

Brighton, as the curious may see in Montpelier Villas. Then to the last of Brighton – Kemp Town – a whole Regency 'new town', which survives intact, and, after years of slumlike decay, is now once more, like Canonbury and Pimlico in London, returning to fashion. Then to the cluster of depressing Victoriana around the railway station, which heralded the end of 'smart' Brighton; and so, on through all the stages of nineteenth- and twentieth-century architecture, the visitor is left free to lament the past or herald the future as he prefers.

Such, then, are some of the attractions offered by Brighton. As I write of them I find it easier to forgive those many detours that buses and taxis make from my London home on the Embankment as we approach Victoria Station. Even London's traffic is forced to change its course because of the queues of summer visitors going to Brighton, as it only otherwise does for the Queen or the Lord Mayor.

South Africa – A visit to my Mother's Land
1961

```
      *
  *       *
      *
```

Many South Africans who for two or more generations have not
been overseas still call England 'home' or 'the old country'. My
claim in reverse is at least as good as theirs, for South Africa
is after all my second home – my Mother's birthplace, where
some fifty members of my family live.

As the Comet sped on the last lap from Salisbury to
Johannesburg I tried to think of myself as South African. I didn't
find it easy. There was so much that I had heard about the Union
in the last years that made me unwilling to accept its claim upon
my allegiance. However, I had come to see and not to judge;
above all, I had come to look at the Whites, their ways of living,
their fears and hopes, to see South Africa through their eyes.

The air hostess broke into these thoughts by handing me the
immigration form. I was ready to be asked whether I was
European, even whether I was White. A recent visit to the
American Southern States had conditioned me to restaurants
and streetcars and lavatories with racial labels. But 'Hebraic'!
I hadn't expected that category. I am of the generation that
cannot easily forget Hitler. However, I must record that of all
the many Jews I afterwards met in the Union, though many
expressed fears of latent anti-semitism, none ever referred to
this racial categorizing laid down by the Union Government.

I had been told that when Mr Randolph Churchill visited
South Africa, he put down his race as 'probably white'. I saw no
way of rivalling this protest.

53

And now I had arrived in Durban, and my family were asking me: Did I find it changed? Changed it was, of course, since 1924; a town would have to be even sleepier and more provincial than Durban that would not have changed in all those years. The centre with its semi-skyscrapers had become the stereotyped downtown of any American town that is not a city. The suburbs spread in all directions.

Here are the gracious homes and gardens of the White population. 'Gracious' now has come to have an ironic ring, so let me say at once that the suburbs of the South African cities really are quite something. The houses are well-designed in materials well suited to the climate – none of those Italianate green-tiled roofs that seem so desolate in winter on our own South coast – and, except in certain rich Johannesburg areas, the owners have avoided Hollywood excesses.

The gardens can hardly miss being splendid with their profusion of flowering trees – scarlet flamboyants and flame trees, pink or apricot hibiscus and a score of others in every season, nor can they easily miss being well-kept where labour is so easily come by.

Gnomes are still to be seen where in England people would 'know better', and in Houghton, a rich suburb of Johannesburg, I saw statues of nude African girls by the sides of deep blue swimming pools which, in the existing racial circumstances, were in such shocking taste that it seemed all right to laugh rather than to be indignant.

*

The interiors of the homes are perhaps not so different from those of the rich suburbs of England, although they seem surprisingly behind American houses in modern devices. Taste, like everything else, is in general a little naïve – *art nouveau* lamps survive unnoticed where an equivalent English housewife would have cleared them away and, at a more sophisticated level, Regency stripes and Spanish ironwork grilles are still thought to be the height of fashion.

54

Snobbery about taste is in poor taste anyhow and, if I make this point at all, it is only to wonder that the well-off South African housewife who subscribes to *The Queen* magazine should fail to catch up with its treadmill demands upon her sophistication. I should like to think that it was because she was finally indifferent to *chic*, but I suspect that it has more to do with the strange love-hate towards England that marks the average English-speaking South African, even in that last outpost of a vanished Empire, Natal.

This is much more interesting than the straight hostility of the Afrikaners. A cultivated Afrikaner professor, en route for Germany, remained on board for the three days that his ship berthed at Southampton. During a pleasant visit to an Afrikaner family, amid all the friendly exchanges, a silent daughter suddenly burst out at me, 'I hated everything I saw in England,' and then, despite the embarrassment of her family, remained obstinately silent again.

These are merely the expression of historical hatred, but what of the expressions of historical disappointment? So often in English-speaking homes I was told grudgingly, 'So the old country's quite prosperous again'; but more usually I was asked how I liked paying all my income away in taxation, or whether men still had to do the washing-up.

Post-war austerity England is what South Africans chiefly like to remember. This attitude leads to an absurd emphasis on English washing-up, or queuing, or bad weather; it makes the success of the Springboks' rugby tour a matter of life and death; it leads to the constant reiteration of the cry 'We're an outdoor people here in South Africa'.

The President of a University, an otherwise very clever man, told me, 'Our Rhodes scholarship boys mature very late. We're not smart alecs here, you know, like the Americans. And, of course, we're an outdoor people. But once a South African chap gets to Cambridge or Oxford *and the weather keeps him indoors*, he often develops into quite a reading man.'

*

For the men, England, like a lot of other things, is a touch 'cissie'. For the women it is above all uncomfortable.

A comfortably off, intelligent woman said, 'I shall tell you how we're on the edge of a precipice and we've got to wake up. But you needn't take any notice of me. So long as I have four or five native servants I've every intention of remaining asleep myself.'

It is the domestic revolution in England that above everything else has cut off the English-speaking South Africans from us. The picture of England they would like to preserve is that of 1923 or so, and even that era perhaps is a little bolshie. As the pressure of Afrikaner Nationalist rule increasingly irks them, as behind that, the bogey of racial violence refuses to vanish however hard they shut their eyes, so England in all its distasteful unfamiliarity becomes a closer reality.

Some younger couples with children have already left to live in England. 'My daughter talks about buying a house and letting rooms off. What a way to spend one's life! Of course, she'll never stick it.' Thus many mothers, I think. 'Going to live in a three-room flat in Kensington! I can't see old Johnnie cooped up like that. My son's an outdoor man, Mr Wilson. As we all are here. It's an outdoor life.' So many fathers, I think.

This determination to look on England's black side in order to enhance the sunshine of Union life often has its absurdities. Said Mrs Professor T., 'I think I should be as unhappy in your affluent England as I was in your austerity England in 1947. They're neither of them the England I know.'

What England indeed do they know? Grey skies, grey fog, a grey life. Never have weather and scenery been exalted as I heard them in the Union. It is true that the Cape is one of the most beautiful scenes in the world and that Durban lies in a lovely setting; it is true that Johannesburg makes up for its ugliness by a perfect climate; but there is something hysterical in the way that these things are vaunted.

'I couldn't bear to leave it,' said Mrs G., looking out over Clifton beach towards Sea Point and Table Bay. 'I keep hoping that if I shut my eyes tight enough, when I open them again Dr Verwoerd will have vanished.' Mrs L. suddenly and dangerously drew her car to a stop on the cliffs overlooking Simonstown and False Bay. 'I don't believe this damned Government *can* take this beautiful Cape away from me!' she cried.

But is all this love-hate of England among the English-speaking simply a dislike of what may be the future's sole alternative? I think, only in part. The division lies so far in the past.

'You people in England are shockingly ignorant of what happens here,' I was told; perhaps we are. 'You English seem to think there is only one minority – the native. Nobody seems to care what happens to the English minority here.'

The basic muddle involved in this statement, namely that the 'natives' are not in fact a minority at all but an unenfranchised majority of three to one, does not make the cry any the less real, but means, of course, that the cry is one of desperate confusion rather than of any legitimate grievance. The same English-speaking South African a moment later will be pointing out that they are 'a tiny minority amidst a vast black population'.

*

To more intelligent South Africans the plain man's cry that the outside world is ignorant of him is a target for ridicule. 'How they dare to complain,' a South African intellectual said to me, 'when they don't know Madrid from Mandalay . . .'

Disappointment with and hatred of England is quite matched by the same feeling for the United States. 'Americanization' of the cities – by which is meant downtown semi-skyscrapers, air-conditioning in stores, supermarkets appearing in the suburbs – is at once vaunted and then apologized for. As an ardent admirer of American life, I found one common remark more unbearably ignorant than any other, 'I think you'll find, Mr Wilson, that we've taken much the best from America

57

without a lot of the vulgarity. And then, of course, we're not so naïve.'

Perhaps more comprehensible, though possibly more dangerous, is the average South African's ignorance of Africa north of the Limpopo. As the natives grow every day more Africa-conscious, so inevitably must the average White become less so.

'I'm afraid,' said Mr K., a cultured businessman, 'that we're sadly deficient in a lot of what Europe has. But then you mustn't forget that we're separated by 6,000 miles of nothing.' Mr J., whose business took him abroad, said, 'I simply hate going by aeroplane now. Every time I fly there's a bit more of Africa lost. It's pretty grim.' And so the world seems to close in on White South Africa, English and Afrikaans speaking alike, and yet they have no common way of living to defend.

The average English-speaking South African's life revolves around business and home. For two generations now they may have been professional men, but increasingly in 'Nat' South Africa they are being squeezed out of advancement in the public service. It is their greatest grievance against the Afrikaners, and it is undoubtedly true. Yet they have woken up to it late. For generations they have been concerned with making money, with saving and investment. Even now, after Rugger or bowls or sailing, it is their favourite topic. As Anthony Delius, the Union's only satirist, says in his poem, 'The Last Division':

Their language is looked after by the Jews, their politics thought out by the Afrikaners, their colleges embalm enlightened views, while they get on with business and gymkhanas.

*

And their wives make lovely homes, producing cultural backgrounds while their husbands produce profits in the cities.

'Come back and see Joan (or Nora or Claire),' Mr P. will say to the visitor, 'she'll take you round the garden, she knows all the Latin names of the things. She'll tell you what sort of theatre we've got, what sort of music we hear, what that artist chappie's name was who painted that lovely sunset over the bay. She'll tell you what all those places were we took colour photos of in Italy two years ago.'

And there indeed she is, ready to dispense scones and sandwiches and tea at almost any hour, or drinks on the stoep, or, let it be said at once, better meals than you'll get in most English homes.

But what about the culture? Is it much poorer than that of the business and professional middle classes in England or America? I'm afraid that it probably is – because, no doubt, of the Union's growing isolation.

Here the very cultivated intelligentsia that I met in Cape Town and Johannesburg will object. But that isn't really the point. There is a vocal intelligentsia, that the ordinary South African knows as the highbrows. And what he cannot believe is that someone can be reasonably alive to the arts and not be a highbrow.

One does find more culture in Cape Town, as Nora from Newlands will tell you. 'Well, I suppose it's only natural because we are the oldest part of the Union, you see.'

The woman without cultural pretensions, outside the small group who may be called the 'highbrows' of South Africa, still lives in a world of morning tea, tennis, swimming, gossip, bridge, dancing, and so on, varied by the occasional charity committee or flag day. And why not? Why not indeed, if she was not playing out her life against one of history's great tragic backdrops, and if, poor woman, she was not conscious every now and again of the strange lurid lights which, playing over her shoulder, give her bridge parties and cocktail times so frightening a dying-sunset glow.

*

Not all the well-to-do English-speaking ladies live in this strange, menaced cloud-cuckoo-land. Mrs L., a businessman's wife, Mrs P., farmer's widow, and Miss J., a doctor's sister, all have reason to object to what I have written, for they are members of the Black Sash, and the Black Sash is, on any count, one of the most remarkable as well as one of the most admirable feminine activities I have encountered.

Hear Mrs L., who is voluble and not without a touch of Roedean jollity, describe it:

'People will tell you we're simply a lot of silly women who ought to be doing our work at home, that we're screaming suffragettes and so on. Of course, we began with shock tactics as a protest against the packing of the Senate – standing about with black sashes on in attitudes of grief whenever Ministers appeared in public.

'Of course, it was a bit theatrical, it was meant to be. It woke people up and shook the Ministers a little too – respectable ladies can be such an embarrassment – but above all it got women thinking. Then the Africans came along and asked, if we were out to underline what was wrong in the country, why couldn't we help them meet their grievances?

'We feed African families where the man is gaoled, we help African women to meet evacuation orders, we go with them to court in pass cases, we protest against job reservation, banishments, Press censorships.'

In fact these ladies with gracious homes are in it up to the neck. They have met the fate of all people who act because their emotions tell them that they must: they have been labelled by the Right as Communists, by the Left as society ladies amusing themselves by doing good.

Mrs L. was well aware of these charges. 'We don't have many poorer women with us, certainly, but quite honestly that's because they haven't the time, and we have.'

Apart from what they have achieved, these Black Sash women alone among well-to-do English-speaking women know what the lives of the 'natives' are like in some degree; they have attended courts with them, waited with them in the long hours of bench sitting which a life of forms and passes issued by an entrenched bureaucracy demands.

They have seen the homes of their servants and the family misery that Apartheid brings. They were the only English-speaking South African women I met who did not seem frightened of the 'natives,' because they knew a little about them. The Black Sash ladies, not afraid to be absurd, not afraid to be emotional, have won back some part of White dignity.

*

But all this is enough about the English-speaking Whites; they are, after all, only one million out of three. The emphasis seems to have been upon the women, but then the men's activities are more circumscribed. As one man said to me, 'We men couldn't really have an equivalent of the Black Sash. The women can do that sort of thing, but you can't let yourself go on like that if you're in business. You don't know what customer you may offend.'

*

And now for the Afrikaners. It is perhaps best to begin by saying that as an Englishman, with only English-speaking connections, it was not at all easy to meet Afrikaner Nationalists. In my family in Natal it seemed almost impossible.

Afrikaners who had left the Nationalist fold were far easier to come by. Many, like one of the most intelligent members of my family, were members of the multi-racial Progressive party. Some young Afrikaners I met had joined the non-racial Liberal party. Recent events have driven a number of younger urbanized Afrikaners from the fold and when they split off they move right out of the Nationalist or even moderate orbit. But their number is few.

At times it seemed as though my English-speaking friends were deliberately trying to prevent me from meeting 'Nats'. The truth is that, apart from business connections, there is for the most part no communication between the two worlds in the lives of ordinary people

It is also true, I suspect, that my English friends wondered how I would stand up to Afrikaner charm, for Afrikaners have great charm, and they have a coherent, traditional life to defend. That they defend their heritage by a system that is intellectually disreputable and only emotionally based does not at first distress one so much as the feeble failure of the English-speaking to evolve *any* policy.

There is something fascinating about the Alice Through the Looking Glass complexity and intricacy of Apartheid schemes. As you are told how this district is being cleared of Coloured and African squatters to make way for Malays, and that that district is being provisionally located to Africans, who will later be moved further out to make way for the Coloureds, you can for a while be fascinated as by some ingenious children's race game. Until, of course, you reflect on what it means in terms of human misery, until you see that in all the fair land of the Cape only the sand dunes of Nyanga could be found to accommodate the corrugated iron sheds of the African working people.

But that is Apartheid in its bureaucratic working. How many happy Afrikaner families know its real meaning in human suffering one can only surmise.

The first contact I could make was with a young intellectual Nationalist, the easiest group to reach. In fact, like a great number of Afrikaner intellectuals at the present time, he had his doubts about the Nationalist policy. This was at a time when eleven intellectual ministers of the Dutch Reformed Church had published their objections to Apartheid as un-Christian, when *Die Bürger*, the Afrikaans Cape newspaper, was objecting to the Nat's treatment of the Cape Coloured community. I met doubts everywhere among the more intellectual Afrikaners, even at Stellenbosch University, the heart of cultural Afrikanerdom. My anti-Nat friends studied these breaks in Nationalist unity every day as Liberals used to descry the simplest words of Goering or Rosenberg in the hope that the 'split' had come at last. The discontent, practical, emotional and doctrinal of many Afrikaner Nationalists for their leader's policy is genuine enough, I am sure, but I remember always a conversation I heard one evening at a party. A Nationalist professor had been telling me how much safer he thought South Africa was than Europe. 'England could be destroyed tomorrow by the first atom attack, but we're out of all that. Our atom attack is simply the blacks and we've got police and an army to keep them down.' His younger disciples sat round, applauding this 'last ditch' attitude, and above all that he was taking the aggressive against an English visitor. 'You English and American chappies can find nothing to do but criticize, but your position isn't so enviable. We've got a way of life and we're not going to give it up because our methods shock you lot.' It was true that they had a way of life to defend and, what was more, they were all skilled men in their professions who believed that their skills would no longer be wanted in a black-dominated South Africa. 'Make no mistake we shall hold on whatever the rest of the world says. The rest of the world was on our side in the African war but that didn't stop the English from imposing their terms on us. We shall hold out until . . .' 'Until what?' I asked. 'Well,' said a very clever young man, 'until, I suppose, something happens.' He laughed. 'I expect you think that shows we've got no hope. But who knows what will turn up? You didn't expect the Sputnik ten years ago, did you?' He saw that I did not find this very convincing. 'Well, anyway you'll be atomized in England by then.' Then, satisfied that they had carried the war against me far enough, they began to emphasize their moderation, their dislike of certain aspects of Nationalist policy and so, 'There'll be changes, Mr Wilson, you be sure of that.' Some English-speaking South Africans moved hopefully at this, the professor swung round on them: 'But not by breaking the Afrikaner ranks,' he shouted, 'make no mistake about that. We shan't break ranks whatever we feel. We're not coming over to your parties. We want changes, but not at that price. Afrikaner-dom, first and last.' 'Yes,' said the younger man, 'you English South Africans are always talking about leaving. You've got somewhere to go. But we Afrikaners have our backs up against the wall. Not even Holland wants us.' It was quite untrue as far as he was concerned. His talents would have commanded a highly-paid job in the United States any day. But he didn't mean himself, he spoke for his poorer brethren, for *Ons Volk*, for Afrikanerdom. As a result I am not very hopeful about the 'great split' in Nationalist ranks.

*

What is this way of life that is the strength and also the insanity of the Afrikaners? An Englishman in such a short time can only get a glimpse. After Afrikaner intellectuals, I cleared the next easiest hurdle – the urbanized Afrikaner business world. The rich Afrikaner businessman of Johannesburg is a postwar phenomenon, a product of South Africa's industrial revolution, for the Union is having its industrial, technological, social and racial revolutions all at the same time. When we think what a mess we made of our industrial revolution on its own, let us hesitate before we criticize them too easily. The few Afrikaner business families that I managed to meet were not so unlike the English-speaking business families. Only one generation back they had come from farming communities that thought commerce was of the devil, so that they wore their urban emancipation with the slightly self-conscious manner of a broadminded clergyman playing poker. Their *braaivlei* (barbecues) are a little more prim, but heartier, more vigorous than the English-speaking cocktail parties. In contrast to the English-speaking, the men hold the floor on all 'cultural' or 'serious' subjects, and at the sound of any such topic Betsie or Anna tends to bustle off to see if the native boy has cut the right sandwiches – it is men's talk. They live more simply, care less about the Joneses, I think, than the English-speaking. If the interior décor in the Afrikaner suburbs of Linden (Johannesburg) or Bellville (Cape Town) is crude, dominated by women's-magazine taste, the gardens were more individual. If the English of Durban live in our Sunningdale, then the

Afrikaners of Johannesburg live in the nicer suburbs of Zurich. Perhaps it will only take a few more years for the differences to vanish, for the Afrikaans urban middle class to shed their primness and develop snobberies. Meanwhile adaptation to urban life is not easy and the incidence of divorce is very high. But of course urban life is not the kernel of Afrikanerdom which reposes its culture on country life. 'We have roots on the soil so we're not touched by the city troubles,' said a Cape Afrikaner. His English-speaking colleague told me that these very Afrikaners were entirely disorientated now they were in a town – 'They don't even know what to do with their honeymoon leave when they're not on the farm,' was how he put it. I was privileged to see a little of Afrikaner farm life near Cape Town. This sounds a pompous way of writing, but privileged is the right word, for like all country life it is very private, though exceedingly hospitable. The pleasant-looking low white farm houses, the vineyards, the wonderful mountain scenery, all conspire to make one friendly towards this simple, traditional way of life. The rather loud-voiced, downright, practical women with their oddly brusque flirtatiousness, their hospitality, their preserved figs and rich home-made tarts have a kind of easiness and a colour that has been sucked out of the English-speaking farmers' wives by gentility, good taste and party manners. The men, too, have an easy boyishness, that strange habit of sudden coarse guffawing that delightfully recalled to me Holland – a country I very much love – and then, they work so hard. Hard work, pride in the local co-operative wine factory to which they subscribe, the weekly visit to the road-houses which are popping up in old Cape homes, the dance or the cinema, the earnest gravity about their duties as elders in the local church. All this is very attractive after the gentilities and banalities of South African suburban life – and all but a little city life in Johannesburg and Cape Town is surely suburban. This Afrikaner farm world – and to a lesser extent the English-speaking farm life – has a great charm, but the other side of the medal is not hard to see – the narrowness, the

65

hardness, the monotony. And if this is so in the Cape, how much more so in the Free State, and how much more so again in the Transvaal, which even the Free Staters call 'wild'. Yet it is to these communities, with many of the farms now denuded of white farmers by the lure of the cities, left to Africans to manage for white landlords, that the electoral system gives the majority voice. Nor is this voice only narrow, it is often, I think, more sly than one at first cares to think. Even in the Cape I was struck by this. We questioned a coloured man by the roadside – how he was paid – £1.5.0 a week and his house, and to this was added wine at 4 a.m., 6 a.m., 8 a.m., 12 noon, so the day's potations went on. The same innocent young farmers whom I had liked so much defended this tottie system vigorously: it was first rate for the health of the coloured men. If they drank too much, became alcoholics, that was not because of the tottie system, but because they drank also at weekends in the towns, a monstrous enormity. An English farmer won my heart by saying characteristically that he was trying to get up football for them instead. But no farmer, English or Afrikaner, said what I am sure he knew was true, that the tottie system was very bad for the coloured men's health, that it was however a cheap means of paying labour, and that also as the coloured men like the method, it would be difficult to get labour without it. I was sorry at this, because I should have liked their primitive simplicity and sincerity to have been as real as it appeared.

*

The most striking difference between Afrikaners and English-speaking South Africans, of course, lies in their attitude to the Non-Europeans. Afrikaners, in general, feel that the English South Africans simply do not understand 'the natives'. It is true that many English-speaking South Africans interpret African behaviour in the most aggressive light. 'You realize,' a business-man said to me, 'that they don't *kiss*. They're not like us, you see. If they ever do kiss it's because they're copying what they've seen on the cinema.' He spoke as a man threatened by such un-Englishness. Again an English-speaking housewife said to me, 'The natives are without natural feelings. A husband and wife don't embrace in public even though they haven't met for months.' Out of these differences in their native servants' behaviour, the English South Africans concoct bogeys of suppressed African violence and cruelty. Yet, in the last resort, their attitude is a very English class one. They can face the idea of accommodating an African middle class, but they dread an uprising of 'the servants'. Quite opposite is the feudal, paternalistic attitude of the Afrikaner. He may well have grown up as a child in the country playing with the native children, certainly with the coloured children of the Cape, though at puberty he will be whisked away from their midst. Afrikaners constantly tell one stories to show how they are all on 'real' terms with the Non-Europeans; for instance an Afrikaner shouting in argument with some English-speaking South Africans that all blacks ought to be slaves and so on, then he sees a young African going by with his arm round his girl's waist. He goes up to the African boy, slaps him on the back, and says, 'Life's pretty good, isn't it?' The boy smiles and says, 'Yes, baas.' The English-speaking South Africans meanwhile stand by embarrassed; they have no easy relationship with the natives. Or again, some Africans come to a farm at Christmas and ask to buy a lamb. 'What money have you got to buy *lambs* with?' shouts the Afrikaner farmer. 'You've come to steal my sheep, haven't you? I'll have the police after you.' And he rails at them for an hour. Then he gives them two sheep as a present. 'Make sure one goes to my old nurse down at the kraal,' he adds. 'How is she? I bet you boys don't look after her.' All this boasted easy, bantering paternalism is, I am sure, very sincere, but, of course, it would be offensive in the extreme to any educated 'native'. The Afrikaner in fact may understand his servants, but he cannot face a world in which he must meet educated African doctors or lawyers. It was this difference, I think, that a coloured school teacher meant when he told me, 'The English patronize, but the Afrikaner can make you feel like a dog.'

This attitude lies deepest no doubt with the least educated Afrikaners. It is with them that 'immorality' – i.e. sexual relations with a Non-European woman – is most usually reported. Hagar, after all, was Abraham's bondswoman. Up to a point he treated her kindly, but he did not treat her with respect. An Afrikaner taxi driver, who took me some distance out of Cape Town, defended Apartheid on the simplest terms that 'the native' wasn't quite the same species as ourselves. Yet it was he who declared that 'the coloured women only want one thing: a child by a white man, and good luck to them'; it was he also, whose eye wandered as he talked of politics. 'See those coloured women,' he said, 'they've got Hottentot blood. You can always tell that when they've got those big rumps,' and he winked as he said it.

The poor white Afrikaners, urban and rural, undoubtedly could not have had it worse in the depression of the thirties, and it is to the Nationalist Government that they owe their allegiance for protecting them now by reserved jobs from Non-European competition; for assuring them that, for the white men at least, the bad old days will never return. A high percentage of these poor whites are railway workers, those that I met seemed much like old-fashioned pre-1940 English working people. With £16 a week, low taxes and very low subsidized rents, they do all right. Though even here there are accident-prone, incapable, or other low-grade people who are only just kept above the colour line. I talked to one very pleasant, unlucky man of this kind. His job was to supervise a gang on the railway. 'But my job isn't a real one.' he said. 'As often as not I spend my time walking about trying to keep myself busy.' His holidays fall on different days to those of his African gang, so that when he is away they work perfectly happily without his supervision, and when they are away? 'Well, I just go fishing,' he said. But he's in a job and he's put over some Non-European labour. He has a white man's status. That is what counts.

This last and least skilled wave of Afrikaners that mark the industrialization of South Africa and the flight from the land are the staunch allies of the Nats. Need for allies and supporters in the many battles now ahead has begun to make strange bedfellows in the Union. As long as I can remember in Natal the Indians have been the target of abuse, the coolie without whose presence the Africans would know their place. Now I found the situation quite changed. 'The Indians,' I was told and it is the simple truth, 'are an excellently educated, intelligent, responsible community.' Again and again at the Durban Club someone would indicate the Indian waiter to me, saying, 'These boys are no fools, you know. We must find a place for them. We understand them here in Natal. The Government talks of them as coolies.' Part of this new concern for the Indians by the English-speaking South Africans is quite genuine; if some compounding has to be made, let it be with the Indian with whom he is familiar. Then again, the Indians are something the Afrikaner has not dealt with and does not understand; *ipso facto* the Englishman does. But a more cynical businessman let one part of the cat out of the bag when he said to me, 'The Indians are no less coolies than they ever were, but we need them now against the native.' The sudden devotion now in Cape Town to the coloureds is a mixture, I think, of a similar genuine proprietary affection – 'How dare the Government push our coloureds around?' – and a wary self-interest – 'The coloureds behaved so well during the trouble in Langa.' The dilemma of the Indian and of the coloured communities is, I think, the most tragic feature of South African life. I shall always recall the look of misery on an intelligent, lively coloured journalist's face, when he asked, 'Do you think the Nationalist Government will stay in power?' It was only slightly less intense than the look of fear which he showed when I suggested that sooner or later African rule must become the order of the day.

*

I can imagine now that the reader will be asking, is all South African life made up of racial politics? Broadly speaking, I think, the answer is yes. When I arrived in Durban I tried to keep the conversation off politics; there were some topics, of course, apart from gossip and gardens, they were the small talk of England – juvenile delinquency (White), ducktails (teddy boys), is professionalism killing sport?, the high divorce rate, the high rate of alcoholism, schemes for easing the traffic blocks, dagga (marijuana) smoking among young people – these were all White-only topics. People whom I met invariably expressed their satisfaction that I was not concerned with politics, we would discuss the current evils I have named with much disapproving clicking of tongues, and then my informant would invariably say, 'Of course, the Nats are to blame . . .', or 'So long as the natives listen to agitators . . .', or 'You must understand that while Smuts was in power . . .' and so on. To be in South Africa today recalled to me all the time the atmosphere in England from 1937 to 1939. It was possible then to hold many political views, but it became increasingly impossible to be non-political without lulling oneself into torpor. That, of course, is what a large number of European men and women do, passing their life in a haze of business, homemaking, sport and social round. But they live a half life. Others again give themselves up to sun soaking, the sea and the beach. An intelligent man said to me, 'The Government can do what it likes – so long as it leaves me the sun to bask in. That's where the blacks'll find me when the blood bath begins.' It is a wonderful land for lotus eating. Yet all these people who opt out of the issues seem half alive. South Africans will resent all this criticism. And they are right. If England were in the same dilemma we should have as many failures, and we should be lucky if we had as many who did so well. A young farmer said to me, 'We're only ordinary after all.' And that also is the trouble – they are ordinary people in an extraordinary situation.

Yet many hundreds are trying to be extraordinary. Whatever their opinions, those who have actively immersed themselves in the situation would not exchange South Africa for England or any other 'nicer', safer place, any more than most of us would have gone to Rio de Janeiro or Sydney or Cape Town in 1937 or 1938. Those who leave the Union are either young couples with children longing for security that will allow them to plan careers, or the over-fifties who are too tired to take up fresh struggles. But again and again young people with no family responsibilities told me, 'We couldn't stand it in England, no one's awake to what's happening here.' They are sure that they are at the centre of the world's problems – too sure, they are interested in nothing outside Africa. But, at least, they have a cause. South Africa is the country to which Jimmy Porter should go, only Dr Verwoerd wouldn't want him. It is essentially not the place for Joe Lampton whom Dr Verwoerd would be so glad to see.

That is why, I think, Johannesburg, which to me, an Englishman nearly fifty, was a rather dreary provincial town trying to be a city, for lively young South Africans is the pulse of all excitement. For here alone perhaps in the Union a young White can move in that intermediate world where the colours mix – a world of crooks and bohemians, social workers and young liberal politicians, a world of all the people whose imaginations and hearts are too large for the colour bar. And here alone, I think, White South Africans really laugh, for all the jokes today are on the side of the blacks. Here are one or two: a young woman told me that when she was cooped up with other European young women in a nursing home, the presence of a man was a thrill to them. One morning they heard a man's step on the verandah. A volunteer went to see who the Romeo was and returned with a disappointed face. 'No man,' she said, 'only a boy. He must have been wearing shoes.' The 'boy' in fact, was a physically splendid African gardener of thirty. Then again an African writer told me that one of his race with great bravery saved two people from drowning near Port Elizabeth. He was awarded £50, but the sum was reduced to £25 when it was found that the second man he saved was an Indian. Again, in the hospitals, I was told, it is the recognized thing that

71

coloured students withdraw when the anatomical subject is a white woman's body. But after the dissection it is an African lab 'boy' who sews up the body and wheels it away. He is only 'the boy' and doesn't count. One could tell a dozen or more such stories. The fun and the vitality is to be seen there among the Africans, with the small boys who improvise jazz on the corner of Eiloff Street, Johannesburg.

That is why my visit to the All-African musical *King Kong* was the highlight of my visit to South Africa. The show is full of vigour and drama; the action takes place in a Johannesburg African township, the liveliest scene in South Africa today. Todd Matshikiza's music is the best of its kind I have heard for years. There are many top moments. The Death Song of King Kong, and, above all, the spontaneously humorous dance of the gumboot boys, which, a moment later, is beautifully parodied by a girl of the chorus. Africans not only laugh but can laugh at themselves. The show stands up as a professional success on its own feet. The performance in Johannesburg was open to members of all races; the University, in whose hall it was shown, is still a multi-racial university, though the Government has now put an end to this anomaly. After moving in the half world where Non-Europeans are shadows on the wall, it was really exciting to sit with a multi-racial audience. The European applause was not patronage, the African applause was not partisanship, both were responding to the genuine laughs and thrills of a first-rate professional performance. It is this show that Dr Verwoerd is allowing to come to London, granting sixty-two passports to African performers – something quite unprecedented and in its own way extremely ironic. But then, if the White South Africans do not have any conscious jokes to make, they often contribute very funny unconscious ones. For example their favourite radio serial – the Mrs Dale of the Union – is called 'So Little Time'.

On a Black Sea Holiday
with Mr K.
1963

*
*   *
*

I have always suspected that my fiftieth birthday would be a day of surprise.

It was – it brought me an invitation to visit Nikita Khrushchev at his country house in Pitsunda on the Black Sea shores.

The invitation, of course, was not to me only, but to a number of Western writers who attended a meeting in Leningrad of COMES, an entirely non-political literary organization founded five years ago by Italian writers.

We had talked very frankly. The old disagreements were there but among some of the Soviet writers, especially the young ones, we found men who talked a language we understood – personal, direct, free from ideological gobble-degook.

*

The Russian hospitality was fantastically cordial. We British got the full benefit of the nuclear test pact.

But a visit to the man at the top we had not expected.

However, here we were in Moscow rising at four in the morning. I am allergic to early rising, yet, from the first moment I saw Khrushchev until we left in the late afternoon, his personality held me completely.

We entered his large estate after a long drive that easily beats the Riviera for lush picture-postcard scenery.

75

I was looking at the pines – the largest in Russia – and almost missed Khrushchev's arrival among us.

Suddenly he was there – exactly and fittingly like a silent-footed, lumbering bear or even more a giant panda.

It was very hot and he wore wide, light-coloured beach trousers and a yoke-necked Russian blouse. No colour in his clothes: his personality provides all the colour that is needed.

Despite his powerful, round face and small, intensely shrewd eyes, he looked shy, almost bashful, among all the strange names and alien political beliefs.

Then he saw Sholokov, the Soviet novelist. His face creased into a wonderful grin and he fell upon his old friend's neck in a hearty Russian embrace. The reserve was over.

Now he took command as he led us politely, but firmly, to his villa overlooking the glorious sea – a villa that is the finest piece of modern architecture I saw in the Soviet Union.

We passed by wonderful beds of sub-tropical flowers that would make even Monte Carlo millionaires envious. The immediate note of the whole villa was of the very simplest luxury. He was evidently delighted with his large swimming pool and its up-to-date gadgets.

He led us all over the small yet spacious house. We glimpsed rooms with small, neat, white-counterpaned beds that might have been in any English boarding-school.

*

At last we came to our meeting room. It was a gymnasium. But we were not expected to use the vaulting horse, I am glad to say. All was talk.

A few words by French and Italian writers and by John Lehmann for England. All emphasized the hopeful side of our talks without glossing over our differences.

Then, with apparent reluctance, our host addressed us. He let us have it. Yes, peace was OK – Conservatives, Liberals, Labourites, Communists, all wanted that. But writing was different, writing was ideas. There the battle was on.

76

We served the Capitalists, the Russian writers the workers. But both sides should keep talking all the same.

*

I had the impression that he suddenly felt we had paid enough for our lunch, for he stopped abruptly. Off we went to bathe from his private beach. And then to eat – and how! Caviar, smoked salmon, bortsch, trout, duck – the lot! And all the wines to go with it.

The informality was complete and most impressive; security measures were discreetly not in evidence. Isolated from interpreters by the informal seating, Khrushchev looked at first shy again, a bit dejected, impatiently tapping the table with a knife. He ate and drank very sparely.

But after a quarter of an hour he was once more laughing and exchanging stories with Sholokov and his other old writer friends. He even called on Tvardovsky, champion of the New Guard, for a poem.

We capitalist writers had to go for our plane before the celebrations were over and no protocol prevented us – we just got up, shook hands and left.

All top men profess informality; few can afford to practise it.

But behind the shrewd eyes, the heavy padding gait, and the sudden disarming grin, one always senses the iron will that controls the destiny of all the Russias.

Russia – What Khrushchev told the Writers
1963

After the decayed late-Victorian splendour of the hotels of Moscow and Leningrad, Khrushchev's Black Sea villa was a welcome vision of modern architectural beauty – luxurious and simple.

The one high-ceilinged, large-sized room of the house served normally, I imagine, for physical recreation. But now the vaulting-horse and other gymnastic equipment were pushed to the wall. We guests – half-a-dozen Western writers, and a good number from Iron Curtain countries who had been meeting in Leningrad – seated ourselves before Mr Khrushchev. The depressing linoleum which lined the floor of the elegant room seemed designed to keep us in our places.

Representatives of Italy, France, England, and Russia spoke very briefly. John Lehmann's speech, on behalf of the English writers, was a model of clarity: a realistic appraisal of the limited success of our meetings. Jean-Paul Sartre declared his disagreement with de Gaulle's refusal of test bans and his certainty that the French people were not on their Government's side.

To all of this Khrushchev listened with polite blankness, allowing himself the minimum of response needed for courtesy – as, for example, a brief yet somehow sternly reproving chuckle when Lehmann recalled the liberal supply of vodka which our Russian hosts had dispensed to us. It was a performance of non-committal listening that impressed me greatly – as though a baby had learned calculation.

81

Then, with a show of reluctance and after much persuasion, he addressed us. He began by noting that peace was one thing, writing quite another. There could be compromises for peace; none in the war of words and ideas. He told us that in any case Rusk, Harriman and Hailsham had come to negotiate only because of the Soviet Union's strength. Cuba had given the Americans a valuable fright.

He illustrated the dangers of the personality cult by reference to Stalin's isolation from the people. Elephants, he told us, are mysterious only if people are not familiar with them. But lest we should suppose that the elimination of personality worship would reduce the Soviet Union's power to produce outstanding men, he pointed out that elephants are not the less with us because we have become familiar with their appearance.

He seemed to feel the need to defend to us his actions during the Hungarian Revolution. He did so by reference to the Austro-Hungarian events of 1919. He also suggested that Tsar Nicholas I had been quite right from his class point of view to send troops for the bloody suppression of popular rising in the Austrian Empire in 1848. A worker who helped to build a prison for other workers could not escape responsibility; so with writers who wrote for capitalists. 'Those writers are you.'

At this point the Polish delegate intervened to say that the Western writers present were not of that kind. Stopped in his flow, our host went off on to other topics – for example, the folly of the Chinese in measuring Communist sincerity by the wearing of rags. The Russian workers had laboured hard and deserved their reward.

If nothing was very unexpected, the delivery always made it seem striking, even through the unsatisfactory medium of interpretation. I have purposely set down my abridged recollection of the speech in a somewhat random order, for what struck me most was that its unity was not one of argument so much as of tone. The tone was firmly set against compromise, even perhaps at times intended to convey a shock, as when he declared that Stalin for all his faults had played a great part in preparing for the present limited atomic *détente.*

Yet the arguments examined closely were by no means all in accord. If the tone was intended to discourage hopes of cultural co-existence, he yet seemed to approve of the meeting of Western and Soviet writers. Indeed, his reception of us at the end of our conference was a striking official recognition of its importance, particularly as he used the occasion for political observations and not for the conventional Soviet denunciation of Western art and literature that I had feared.

*

What then had been the value of the conference which preceded our unexpected invitation to the Black Sea? I should say at once that this was my first visit to the USSR; that my books have never been translated into Russian and that such stray references to them as have come my way from Soviet publications have been hostile. The other English novelist who attended the conference was William Golding, whose works also have not been translated into Russian. The pessimistic tone of his fine novels might be expected to be as unsympathetic to orthodox Soviet ideology as my own social analysis and the freedom with which my novels treat sexual unorthodoxies.

Among the French delegates were Alain Robbe-Grillet and Nathalie Sarraute, whose experimentalism of form and relative obscurity cut across the whole Russian concept of popular art. There was also present Magnus Enzensberger, the brilliant young poet and critic from – of all countries – West Germany. That we all of us spoke absolutely freely among audiences that contained Soviet writers of all kinds is, I think, the first and most important achievement.

I have no doubt whatsoever that the conference aroused very great interest and encouraged the less orthodox among the Soviet writers. It would be false to speak of these as only the young writers, since two of the most encouragingly open-minded Russian speeches of the conference came from Ilya Ehrenburg, aged 72, and Alexander Tvardovsky, aged 53.

Yet there is a degree, as I found in private conversation as well as in listening to speeches, to which only the younger writers speak that personal, direct language unencumbered by metaphysical jargon with which we English writers are familiar. It is also true, as I found in private conversation, that the oldest generation, who knew Mayakovsky and Babel and Gorky, have made a real link in the new young writers, and that these generations speak to each other, especially in humour, over the heads of the official middle-aged.

None of this means to say that these less orthodox writers are not Communists, only that their approach to the arts is not monolithic but varied and personal.

Confessions of a
Zoo Lover
1964

```
      *
  *       *
      *
```

I am an inveterate haunter of zoos. No opportunity is
neglected, from whole rambling days spent exploring the
landscape and the rare animals of foreign zoos when I am
abroad on business or holiday, down to short purposeful visits
to the London Zoo near my home, to watch exotic favourites
like lemurs or to gain refreshment from the familiar beauty of
the flamingos. Most people seem to find this zoophilia rather
eccentric. That wasn't always so. When I was a small boy my
hobby was very popular with my parents: zoos are convenient
places to pack children off to for the afternoon. It was only in
my teens, when my love for zoos became more instead of less
ardent, that my parents showed signs of alarm. Faced with an
unconventional son, their principal anxiety was: 'What will the
boy do when he grows up?' All my friends, all my interests were
judged by whether they would help me to a 'suitable' career.

Where did this passion for wild animals fit in? For my
urbanized parents it offered only visions of a uniformed zoo
keeper carrying buckets of horse meat to the hungry lions, or
buckets of lion dung to some place unspecified. Neither activity
spelled the sort of career that ambitious British middle-class
parents have in mind for their sons. If only we had known some
distinguished explorer or naturalist, preferably one who had
been knighted, my parents might have seen the whole thing
differently. I wish that we had. It would have been both
'suitable' and exciting to have been the director of a vast

national zoological park. However, I shouldn't have minded if I hadn't risen so high: I should have been content to have been the humblest stuffer of exhibits at the Natural History Museum. Anything to do with wild animals – for my interest in them has grown, not diminished, with the years.

I suppose there are a lot of grown men who love wild animals – men, that is, who are not professionally concerned with them. I don't see too many on my visits to zoos. Of course there are always fathers of families, or uncles taking out nephews and nieces: and there is the immense popularity in England of television features about zoos or wild life; but these are mostly for family viewing. Wild animals shouldn't be studied in the company of children, or only in order to study the children's reactions. And even then there are dangers that the adults will spoil the children's pleasure; most grown-up people seem unable to resist using animals in order to show off before children. They moralize, or they instruct, or they patronize, or they indulge in sub-Disney whimsy, or, worst of all, they make facetious remarks about the animals' natural habits.

Children usually receive all this with scorn, but that doesn't deter the grown-ups, for so many people need to protect themselves from the very probing questions about human existence that the sight of wild life arouses in most of us; to guard themselves from the sudden visions, often beautiful and always absorbing, of a way of being alive so different from ours that it can make human life seem clumsy or absurd; above all they have to hide from themselves the realization of what man's mastery – so constructive in art and science – has done to destroy other forms of life that have not so easily adapted to co-existence with his own. Inane chatter and silly laughter can protect us from the vision; to receive it, we need quiet and an alert attention.

*

We must wander about zoos, especially those we don't know already, without guides or maps or fixed programme. This is the only way to come without warning upon something strange, something previously unknown. So it was that, skirting a great oak tree in one of the many winding avenues of the Hagenbeck Zoo in Hamburg on a leafless, frosty, but sunlit February afternoon, I saw suddenly a strange, fat, purplish blue nose thrust toward me from out of the surface of a rocky pool. It *was* a nose, yes, and thick lips that bristled. For the moment I thought that a stout city burgher had fallen into the icy water and was breathing his cardiac, purplish last before my very eyes. It was only then that the heavy, creased, sleekly furred body rolled over in the water, and I caught a glimpse of tiny deep-set eyes and short yellowish tusks. I knew that I had seen my first walrus.

As I watched the heavy yet sinuous creature roll over and over I saw that the covering fur was brown, and the bristly nose and mouth, creased and pricked like a pepper pot with little holes, were really a rather ordinary darkish gray. I stayed and watched the walrus consume a meal of small fish (not, alas, of the clams that his great bristly moustache cleans). As I watched the walrus, it took its place in my mind with the other animals of its order, somewhere between the graceful, lively and doglike sea lions and the gross, bottle-nosed sea elephant. It was evidently delighted by the ice-edged pool at Hagenbeck's that wintry afternoon, recalling no doubt its Arctic home.

Yet the sudden freak of sunlight which had shown me the walrus' head coloured a purplish blue has left its mark with me, in the form of nagging, irrational doubt whether the creature is so well adapted to North Pole conditions as is generally supposed.

Unpreparedness can also illuminate the nature of some animal that has previously aroused no response. So it was with tapirs. I was familiar with them from my childhood visits to the London Zoo – both the brown Brazilian species and their cousins from Malaya whose hindquarters are banded with grayish white as though enveloped in dirty bathing towels.

They had always disappointed me; they were housed in a dusty pen between the elephants and the hippopotamuses, and their long noses seemed such feeble efforts after the elephants' trunks. Then, too, I could always hear the slopping of water against the walls of the next pen; if I did not hurry on I should perhaps miss those great pink open jaws with their stubs of yellowing teeth, and the little eyes on stalk-ends malevolently glaring, as the hippos surfaced above the muddy, steamy waters of their pool. With such alternative attractions, I had no time for tapirs. It was not until I visited the Fleishhacker Zoo at San Francisco one late October morning that I realized how enchanting and individual these creatures are. The fog which had so infuriatingly spoiled my views of the pelicans and sea lions as I had come up the coast still persisted that morning at the zoo. Yet the weather, at any rate to an Englishman, seemed very warm for late autumn; suddenly the white mists blew apart and before me to my surprise was a large enclosure with a pool in which some graceful but rather small, plump, Marc-like brown horses were bathing themselves with evident delight. As I watched them through the clearing mist I wondered not only why horses should be on show like this, but also why they should seem, almost pig-fashion, to wallow – and wasn't there something more than Marc-like, almost pure surrealist, about their noses? They were, of course, Brazilian tapirs. No longer set in the sad, dusty pens of the London Zoo as a foil to their more exotic-looking African neighbours, but given their own trees and scrub and pool, the tapirs seemed to offer one of the most direct visual links (there is, of course, no zoological connection) between the wild and the domestic, between the rain forests of South America and horses rolling on their backs or frisking in farm meadows on a sunny day.

You must see tapirs bathe to watch them in their relaxation. And it is a relaxed animal that is most rewarding, from the plunging dolphins of Marineland to the penguins in their rookery at Edinburgh, where birds are bred for other zoos. Crowded, cramped conditions, like human slums, produce only torpid, slow-witted creatures. It is only some of the reptiles, particularly crocodiles or alligators, that seem to me a more effective spectacle in crowds, when one great scaly body totters in slow articulated jerks over another, or a small vicious eye flicks suddenly alert behind some other creature's cruelly spiked tail. The deadly inertia, the sly murderous intent of alligators seems to need that hot and stifling air, that sweet corrupt smell that only comes from the fly-blown, unhygienic conditions of small commercial snake gardens such as I remember to have met with off the highroads of Louisiana.

Great tortoises, too, best reveal their slow wrinkled agelessness in some crowded, dusty paddock. The sight of one of these monsters climbing over the vast circumference of another's shell, the brittle nails of one huge, sagging, fleshy foot tapping its slow-motion ascent while another foot drags slowly up behind it, seems at first an appalling irreverence to great age. I have watched these tortoise scenes and I have now come to see the disregard of these ancient creatures for one another's dignity as the supreme height of apartness, of old age's in-difference. It is easy indeed to summon up the pathetic fallacy when watching tortoises or turtles. Who can see the great turtles swimming around one another in some aquarium tank, who can observe their slow curved flippers and their pouting, parrot-beaked mouths, without feeling that they are an embodiment of incurable melancholy, a funeral wake under water? It is not only reptiles, however, that are especially rewarding under zoo conditions. It was, of course, exciting to have a green parrot's sudden flight shown to me in the African bush, but this flash is more a thrill than a thing of beauty; it cannot compare with the chattering, shrieking clash of violent colours that any zoo parrot house offers to the visitor. I saw last summer my first hummingbird at large, darting among the flowers in the garden of a Canadian bishop. So that large bee, I realized, was a hummingbird; but I cannot pretend that this single bird had the beauty of the glittering greens and golds and crimsons that flit from one beaker of condensed milk to another

91

among the tropical plants of the London Zoo's hummingbird house.

Nature is not always second best. I have seen many delightfully-designed flamingo pools but none has ever equalled the beauty of the sudden flash of rose and gold as a flock of flamingos took off a hundred yards from me against the sun in France's Camargue nature reserve. To see a new animal or to notice a familiar one for the first time, to see animals in conditions that seem exactly to reveal their inner natures or to give oneself up to the colour and shape alone, these are some of the pleasures of zoo visiting and they need no human companion. I remember in the Paris zoo how a friend once spoiled an important zoo-going moment for me. As we approached a newly-built round house, deep and terrifying roars that had in them a magnificent growling note came to us in quick succession. 'Ah, the lions!' said my friend. But I knew it was no lion. The roars were soon mixed with a mad violent hammering against metal. I guessed rightly that what we heard was a gorilla. Now I think that when the gorilla stands on all fours, with its great black muzzle forward, it is the most magnificent creature in the world, a mixture of lion and primitive man in full pride; sitting on its haunches, it seems to me a pathetic attempt to reproduce a human being. Sure enough, in the house there was a large male gorilla, pacing on all fours the length of its large cage, then pausing to roar and pound upon its cage bars in a rage more daunting and yet more splendid than anything I had ever seen in the animal world. I stood in silence. And then my companion said, 'Oh dear, they never sit up when you want them to.' No, zoos are to be seen alone. Only then will you be rewarded with those sudden glimpses, those sudden revelations of what it must really be like to feed as anteaters do with their long sticky tongues, or to see life only as a side view as birds do; to swing from branch to branch in ever faster capers like a gibbon, or to watch the world upside down in slow motion like a sloth.

*

What is the best kind of zoo? The answer seems so easy: the one which most exactly reproduces the natural conditions of the animals. But this simple answer, like most simple answers, is very misleading. Vast countries like the United States, Africa and Australia have their Yellowstone, Kruger, Serengeti and other national parks, where indigenous fauna can be preserved and seen in their own ecology. In the nineteen thirties it seemed likely that they would eventually supplant the old-fashioned zoos. Events in Africa give the lie to this assumption. Paradoxically, just as Europeans and Americans are on the threshold of such easy air travel that the New Yorker or Londoner may soon be able to refresh himself at will with the sight of the lions drinking at dawn in Kruger or Serengeti, at this very moment African governments are taking over, and for them better living standards for their peoples have priority over game preservation. It is hard to disagree with them; every bit of good African land will be needed for cultivation if the African people are to live decently. In any case, for all but the urbanized Africans wild life means food. In the zoos of Pretoria and Johannesburg I have seen Africans from 'up country' fascinatedly watching a mother giraffe with her young foal, or laughing at the antics of a baboon. For the young children the pleasure was an easy one, but for the old grandfather it was obviously strange, almost embarrassing to be watching something that should really be shot. I have seen exactly the same reactions from a group of Serbian peasants peering into the wolf pit of the zoo that has been so beautifully made in the medieval walls of Belgrade, and from an old Tuscan shepherd who was being shown the fine collection of wild boars in Rome's zoo by his sophisticated grandchildren. It takes a long time to unlearn an inherited attitude to animals. As yet the Africans can hardly afford the lesson. By the time they can it may well be too late; African need will have completed the extermination started by the greed of white sportsmen. The sheep-farming needs of Australia are hardly less menacing to that ancient world of marsupial life. One can honour and support the many voices of royal persons and famous naturalists raised to save the game reserves, but one can hardly believe that time is with them.

In many parts of the world wildlife reserves are surely a thing of the past. The future is with what once seemed obsolete – the zoos. Zoological gardens all over the world, even the old-established zoos like those in London or Hamburg, have ceased to seem the fusty, unsanitary relics of medieval menageries that disapproving, hygienic-minded, forward-looking parents (not, thank God, my own dear backward-looking, closed-bedroom-window Victorian parents) used to think them in the twenties and thirties; on the contrary, zoos are of the future. And to visit a good few of them – San Diego, for instance, or the rebuilt zoos of Berlin or Frankfurt-am-Main – is to find modern zoo directors well aware that the survival of life's variety is in their hands; they are using all the modern discoveries of medicine, hygiene, engineering and architecture to present their Noah's arks in the most imaginative ways possible. These new zoos make me seriously doubt whether vast national parks or what are sometimes called open zoos are necessarily superior. In the nineteen thirties the London Zoological Society developed an additional park outside London, at Whipsnade, in the typical southern English countryside of the Chiltern Hills – rolling, grassy downland with chalk quarries. I remember my intense excitement at the idea of this new zoo, the first English zoo of 'natural conditions', the first zoo without bars. My first visit was a great disappointment. If the idea was to give the inmates greater liberty, then it had been achieved; but if it was to suggest their native setting, then the English country background hampered the imagination far more seriously than the houses and sheds of their London paddocks, which in any case were necessary in our climate. And the real disappointment was to realize that the smaller mammals, the reptiles, the insects and the birds either had no place in such a 'free' zoo or were to be kept under conditions that were no whit better than the houses and cages of the conventional nineteenth-century zoological gardens. I think my first visit to this open zoo at Whipsnade almost destroyed my zoo-loving, for it seemed to suggest that there was no real progress possible for zoos. Indeed, faced by a choice between this diminished and artificially 'natural' reserve and the elegantly-laid-out Victorian gardens in Regent's Park, London, I preferred the older institution, even though the crowded conditions and the high smells in many of the houses still suggested all too directly the squalid, brutal medieval menageries from which zoological gardens are descended.

Postwar zoos have shown that this choice is not a real one. To begin with, bars and wire mesh are a thing of the past, but it is not only the large carnivores that can now be seen openly, across ditches and moats; beams of light have now become the invisible barrier that allows us to move among tropical birds or to watch reptiles by their streams without the frustration of glass or wire. Nocturnal creatures too, round-eyed owls and pottos, the mysterious visaccia, the bushbabies – all these can be induced to lead their active life in the daytime, by doubling the electricity at night-time and so literally turning night into day. Almost any effect of climate can now be created artificially, and there is no need to pretend that the English hills are the proper setting for kangaroos or the redwoods of California the perfect background for European wolves.

Of course in the continents which still have a wide variety of wild fauna, use will be made of the natural settings; but for the future I believe that zoos will give us individual houses that reproduce ideal conditions for the creatures within them: houses that not only provide a spectacle for the visitor unclouded by bars and wire, but also make possible for the animals the necessary withdrawal to solitude that will allow them to mate and breed in peace. Yet the parks in which the houses are placed will not, I believe, attempt to represent 'natural conditions'; they are far more likely to return to ornamental parks like those of the beautiful zoo at Lisbon, recalling the aristocratic origins of zoos as noblemen's pleasure gardens. This, of course, means a revival of zoos in the centres of cities, not only small collections like those in New York's Central Park, but the large elaborate zoos like those of Antwerp or Barcelona where only the occasional crash of brakes or the rattle of an electric train makes you realize that you are not, after all, far away in a limitless garden of Eden, but in the heart of a modern industrial town.

Oddly enough, natural surroundings are most effective in the world of fishes and marine mammals. The Oceanariums at Marineland and Durban give real samples in depth of the life of the Pacific and Indian oceans, and beside them the old-fashioned, though excellent aquaria at Monte Carlo and Naples give a very limited, magic-lantern view of the seas. Space, however, will probably always remain the final bar to any wholly inclusive Noah's ark. Walruses are being slaughtered to the verge of extinction, yet, although so far they are not easy to keep in captivity, one or more specimens will always be found at the Bronx Zoo, or at the Hagenbeck Zoo at Hamburg; many species of whales are equally threatened, but it is difficult to see how the largest of these will ever be preserved in captivity. The home area of most wild animals in nature is comparatively limited, so that under modern zoo conditions the lion or the giraffe does not suffer because of some degree of confinement, and with modern veterinary medicine and feeding it lives a good deal longer and more happily than in a wild state; but the birds of prey – the eagles and the condors – still flap at the top of their vast cages in even the most modern zoos – the last remnant of that cruel confinement the bear tied by its leg in the pit, from which the useful, humane and beautiful modern zoos descend. For city dwellers in Philadelphia, New York, or Berlin, or for small nations with an ever-shrinking countryside like England or Holland, the zoo is increasingly the only means left of learning some respect and humility before other than human ways of living; the only means of learning pleasure in the existence of what is not the

96

same as ourselves, and so perhaps learning more tolerance of other human beings with different noses, colours or smells.

*

As the wild areas of the world gradually disappear, we may establish our Noah's arks in which to study the movements and habits, breeding, longevity and diet of various species, both for our material good and for our spiritual refreshment. We may find conditions that will save from extinction those Australian primitives, the duckbill platypus and the echidna; we may find substitutes for the bamboo shoots of the panda, the termites of the aardvark, the rain forests of the okapi and the heathland of the Scots grouse; but bit by bit we are changing them also.

Gradually as one species after another breeds successfully in captivity our zoos are becoming self-replenishing. Veterinary medicine eliminates zoo diseases as our own medicine combats human ills. We no longer depend on nature for the animal world. The porpoise, thanks to Miami and Marineland, is added to our domestic pets. The new lighting and showers and kitchens and gymnastic kit for gorillas and orang-utans in modern zoos resemble the facilities provided for prize-fight champions. It is confidently said that changed conditions will affect the smaller wild cats – the genets, the ocelots, and the pumas – and make them friendly, lively and lovable instead of torpid balls of fur that are apt to fly into sudden spluttering rages. Lynxes and dingo dogs, famous for their untamable ways, can be transformed by chlordiazepoxide into the friendliest of creatures. By the time nature's wild life has been destroyed by the spread of towns and farms, the zoo animals may well have become domestic pets. Then once again uncle and auntie can begin their patronizing whimsy, for domestic pets are notoriously receptacles for the exhibitionism and the surplus egoistic affections of their owners. By that time zoos will have defeated their own purpose. Man will have remade the animal world in his own likeness. I am glad to say that I shall be dead.

The Channel Islands
1961

*
* *
*

In the first years of this century a relation of mine became involved in a doubtful financial deal that might have landed him in jail. Luckily no charge was ever laid. Yet even twenty or so years later, when I was a child, the affair was discussed in my family with a certain shocked pleasure. The story always ended 'how very lucky that the Channel Islands were there for him to go to until it all blew over'. To my youthful imagination the Islands presented themselves as some sort of medieval sanctuary, only especially adapted for 'modern' families like my own who 'did not believe in going to church'. This picture of an up-to-date asylum for outlaws appeared to have little connection with the other picture of the Channel Islands that was familiar to me from my parents' conversation. Periodically, when they discussed the iniquities of income tax – and this, being South Kensington residents living on a small unearned income, they did every day – my Mother would exclaim boldly, 'There's nothing for it but to go to the Channel Islands.' Then she would add that dear Colonel Someone or charming Major Somebody Else found living there so cheap and so pleasant, and the standard of bridge very high. My Mother, having left her native South Africa early to marry, could adopt this Mrs Micawber-like sang-froid about emigration. But my Father, though habitually optimistic, was far too wedded to Sandown and to Tattersall's, to Twickenham and to Lord's, to contemplate departure from England with Mr Micawber's bravado. 'I'm not going climbing over rocks looking for seagulls' eggs with any damned retired colonel,' he would say, and the scheme would once again be shelved. To fugitives from the law and ornithological colonels, I had to add the familiar products – Guernsey tomatoes, Jersey cream, Jersey potatoes, and, that more exotic product, Lily Langtry, the Jersey Lily, whom my father always deprecated as 'a cold piece of goods'. It was a strange and fascinating mixture. I think that I then forgot the Channel Islands for many years, until in 1950 or so a lady in a train recommended them to me for my holiday, saying that they were 'like France without all the bother'. Finally, quite recently at a cocktail party two fellow guests objected to the Channel Islands, but on entirely opposing grounds. The one said that they were 'frightfully up-stage, full of millionaires and duchesses'; while the other described them as 'simply awful. Everybody's char goes there for her holiday now.' I knew that it could not be long before I should have to find out for myself what they were really like. They turned out to be a fascinating maze of entangled social paradoxes.

*

England itself, God knows, with its tail-ends of the past and its first threads of the future inextricably twined together under the pressure of its small island compass, is enough a sociologists' paradise. But the Channel Islands have a good part of these same social problems to solve, with some others of their own beside, and all this in six inhabited islands, the largest of which, Jersey, is no more than forty-five square miles, the smallest of which, Jethou, could reasonably be described as a very large rock. Take the millionaire population of the Bahamas, the country gentry of Norfolk or of Wiltshire, the retired service officers of Cheltenham, the nurserymen and smallholders of Essex, and confine them all to an area half the size of Rutlandshire. For half the year let loose upon them the holidaymakers of Clacton, as well as that 'quieter' type of seaside visitor who seeks a 'family resort' (and a good handful of the new Costa Brava type of English tourist to taste); let the whole (though by no means all the parts) be richer than the Islands have ever known in their history, yet be sure that this new affluence is sufficiently precarious to create a sense of threat. Here you have the recipe for the present social set-up in the Channel Islands.

It sounds an explosive mixture; and indeed beneath the prosperous exterior there are considerable tensions and contradictions in life as lived in Guernsey or Jersey. The very rich who have fled from high-taxation England must be reminded of it each summer as they hear the working-class holiday crowds noisily celebrating their new affluence. For the ex-African administrators, too, driven upon the Islands' rocky shores by the winds of change, the same holiday crowds symbolize an England 'impossible' to retire to 'if you want to spread yourself a bit on your pension'. Yet for these ex-Empire men and their wives, whether from India or Africa, the 'millionaire refugees' from death duties and surtax also suggest an England intolerably outside their means and their remembrance. The greenhouses and chimneys that are the Guernsey tomato-growers' tools of life do not embellish the countryside either for rich English settlers or for typists on holiday. Wealthy English *émigrés* don't help to keep land values within the reach of the prospering young Jersey farmer. Above all, for all classes of 'residents', the shopkeepers and the hotel owners seem to be sacrificing the islands to money values in their desire to attract 'anyone' to the place who is willing to spend. Undertones of all these conflicts and many more come to the visitor, but usually only undertones; especially if the visitor is, as I was, a writer, for the Channel Islands on the whole have had a poor deal from the sociologically inquiring journalist in the post-war years. They have, I think, a good case for resenting the way they have been treated.

To begin with, the Channel Islands are and, no doubt, always have been a sitting target for the armchair moralist. Their geographical isolation, their relatively barren soil, their situation until after 1815 or later between two rival nations have meant that life was very tough for the Islanders and yet also, like all border peoples, there were rich possibilities for the quick, resourceful, not over-scrupulous among them. They had to be 'fly' about taking advantage of the inefficiencies and loopholes of the English or Continental systems from which at best they might hope for a crumb of legitimate trade to live upon. The respectable, the hardworking and the socially responsible Islanders have always tried to build up an economic way of life that would be coherent and stable – cod fisheries, knitting of 'jerseys', cider, shipbuilding, stone quarrying. All were hard and precarious livings, and all through one chance or another eventually dried up. The more 'fly' professions of pirate, privateer and smuggler were no doubt as hard and they, too, have each in their turn disappeared; but, while they flourished, the going was often very good for those who followed them. Not a little of the social position and comparative wealth of the old Channel Islands families who are now fighting to preserve the decent traditional Island way of living came from these less respectable sources. The succour or asylum given to the tax-evading individual or company from welfare England is exactly on all fours with those romantic individualistic occupations of the past; and if, today, evasion of England's fiscal system is one of the most lucrative aids to the Channel Islands, it is ill-becoming for us to moralize about people who for the first time in their history are 'having it really good'. If we object so much, we have the simple remedy of revising our own laws. Of course, it is the case that television social commentaries like *Panorama* and *Tonight* tend to comment on England's social iniquities or absurdities and leave the central conventional way of life as understood; this is the nature of documentary journalism. Applied to a small community like the Channel Islands, however, the effect of this sort of highlighting is far more devastating because the absurd or the socially monstrous appear total rather than partial. For this reason neither Chris Chataway nor Alan

Whicker seem to be remembered in Jersey with any strong affection.

Despite their understandable caution with inquisitive visitors, people in the Channel Islands do reveal the underlying tensions and hostility both between the different social groups and between the different islands. Yet what finally impressed me was that such tightly-packed, ill-assorted groups should manage to live as easily side by side as they do. There are many factors that account for this social cohesion. The Channel Islanders themselves, I think, have an exceptionally stubborn, persistent temperament akin to that of their Norman peasant cousins. It would be untrue to say that they are adaptable to new ways – the older generation of Jersey and Guernsey farmers clearly put up more than the normal farmers' resistance to improved methods of agriculture – but they are long accustomed to ignoring inconvenient changes around them, as, for example, they managed to ignore many aspects of the German occupation. The waves of English immigrants and tourists who have descended upon them since 1840 or so are more a convenient ground for pleasurable grumbling than for any real resentment. If the Norman peasant is stubborn, he is also acquisitive. The Channel Islanders have now the opportunity of making good money and they are willing to suffer many social inconveniences and changes to do so. Farming, cheap organized holidaymaking, gracious living without death duties, colonial pension retirement with low taxation – these may be contradictory, incompatible ways of living – but they are far from incompatible sources of revenue or of income so long as they can be accommodated together. I have sought in vain for exact figures of the three sources of revenue in Jersey and Guernsey – tourism, company and income tax from immigrant residents, and agriculture. One of the principal reasons for their being unobtainable is, in fact, that so many Channel Islanders derive their income from all three or at least from two of these sources. Prosperity makes people very tolerant of their neighbours. The wealthy English who are evading death duties, the retired English colonial servants who can live more graciously upon lower income tax, have also strong incentives to put up with inconveniences. Yet here also a national characteristic comes to their aid: the immigrants have the English infinite capacity for dividing up into mutually exclusive sets without ostentatious avoidance; so that as one woman, who had been telling me about the 'impossibility' of three-quarters of the population of Jersey, was able to say, 'but, thank God, one never sees them about'. As for the seaside holidaymakers – who on holiday sees more of native life than the quaint aspects to which his attention is directed? And if a tourist does glimpse Lady B., or perhaps, more familiar from today's gossip columns, Mrs C., the wife of the famous merging director; and nudges her friend, the momentary contact will be as gratifying to Mrs A. or Lady B. as it is to their admirer. The English do not shed their snobbery with their clothes when they are on holiday. Yet all this ability to get along together, this willingness to put up with irksome or competitive neighbours is a toleration based on material self-interest or social exclusion. And why not? Why not indeed – it would be priggish interference for a visitor to ask more for the Islanders than they ask for themselves. Yet I did meet a number of people – lawyers, farmers, teachers, doctors, tradesmen – who, though they would resent outside criticism, expressed grave anxiety about the underlying malaise of life in Jersey and Guernsey – not just for any particular section, but for the community as a whole.

Their diagnoses, of course, differ, as do their remedies. Is the emigration from Jersey and Guernsey of all under middle age, especially of any youth with skills or a high IQ, a good or a bad thing? Excellent said the optimists. Let them broaden their outlook and return to enrich their native islands as experienced professional men or technicians. But will they return? And can places of any independent entity exist almost without a youth? And what becomes of the less skilled youth that remain behind if they're the only representatives of their generation? Are the Channel Islands in fact becoming another Eire? This is only one set of questions that arose wherever I talked to intelligent, patriotic Jerseymen or Guernseymen. All these questions had a hard element of material, economic urgency in them, but all of them edged off into wider fields of loss of personal or communal identity and of inadequate human satisfactions. The answers, too, as so often today, were confused by the rapidly changing shape of world affairs. Should the Channel Islands cease clinging to their vestiges of traditional customs and laws, should they jettison their bilingual inheritance? Do these things remain only as 'quaint' vestiges to satisfy the affections of the traditional-minded, to create a museum spectacle for visitors? Do the Channel Islands need to find their identity by merging with England, and, if so, should it be with the Welfare State stream of England, or with the Free Enterprise stream? Or could it be that the old 'traditionalists' have by the swing towards Europe become the forward-minded progressives of Island society? Such questions themselves, of course, are always argued in the context of particular economic, practical affairs. Does the traditional Guernsey or Jersey way of life impede the spread of modern skills and techniques in the Islands? Does the 'museum' aspect of Channel Island life, its carefully preserved, much publicized historically separate identity constitute one of the main attractions for tourists, or is the modern tourist indifferent to, if not contemptuous of such folklore quaintness, so long as he gets good bathing with good modern hotels? It may be said that such questions could be asked about a hundred English seaside towns or country districts in the social revolution of our time, but the Channel Islands, assimilated though they are rapidly becoming to post-war English life, do remain more than an agglomeration of districts and towns cut off from the mainland by a short air flight. They have a historical, linguistic and institutional identity that is their own. No doubt this identity could be fairly rapidly destroyed, the absorption could be made as complete as that of Wales or Scotland, though even there the German occupation suggests that geography does still make their case unique. But if this unification were carried through, it could hardly be cemented by any solid industrial, commercial or agricultural tie. All the links between the Islands and the mainland have an impermanent quality – tomato and flower growing are threatened by the European Common Market, death duty *émigrés* and limited companies from England could disappear if there were a violent political swing to the left in English elections or if the Conservatives were able materially to reduce death duties; holiday crowds swarm to the Channel Islands now as they have never done before because flying is becoming a mass habit, but that mass habit may soon take even the least venturesome far further south. This does not mean that Channel Island life is any more threatened in the present upheaval of European life than any other Western European area; certainly not that the Islanders are less equipped with tenacity, adaptability and charm to deal with the coming changes. But a people without a clear identity will necessarily be a confused, disorientated group. In any case I have made my observations on the dilemma of Channel Islands social life in the general belief that unusual, particular patterns of society, unless they can be shown to be actively harmful or mere folksy whimsies, should be strengthened where possible. If only because their preservation is one more victory in the battle for our increasingly threatened human diversity.

One of the peculiarities, the virtues and also the difficulties of the Channel Island problem is that fierce economic competition in the past and dangerous navigation have given each of these small islands an isolated history and therefore a completely different character. It is indeed only possible fully to consider the future of the Channel Islands when one has examined each separately. Since scenic beauty and land value are the main bases of their economy, it is possible to know quite a little about the islands simply by looking at them.

*

The smaller islands, for obvious reasons, present less complicated problems. Chance allowed me to visit both Sark and

Alderney in the most appropriate weathers. Sark has all the surprise of a charming manor house hidden behind grim battlements – massive steep cliffs, a precarious, improbable harbour, a long winding uphill road to the centre; but when you get there, particularly on a hot, sunny November day as I did when no holiday crowds were about, you could be, not on a small rocky island in a dangerous sea, but in a very beautiful and secluded corner of the Cotswolds. Particularly is this so in the seventeenth-century stone house and walled gardens of the Dame, Mrs Hathaway. What it may be like in full tourist season, with so very many visitors a day, I don't know. Mrs Hathaway assured me that the tourists were hardly noticeable, but then someone living in a small walled manor house near Burford or Broadway might say the same. Nevertheless, as she pointed out, it is true that holidaymakers tend to congregate in the much advertised beauty spots. At any rate this feudal-ruled island, where motor traffic is forbidden, is geared entirely to the tourist trade – a few regular family parties living in, so to speak, and the great mass coming on day trips from Guernsey. Save for a few ugly bungalows of the 'twenties and 'thirties, the Dame has preserved the appearance of the island most successfully. There is always that feeling of being away from it all even in a crowd, largely because there are no cars and because one must wait for the next boat to get back to St Peter Port.

The people of Sark, the Dame told me, know that the island depends for its livelihood on being a museum and they sensibly keep it that way. I have no doubt that Mrs Hathaway herself is the able architect of this unified tourist economy, for besides the formidable 'grande dame' charm with which she so successfully and bravely managed the occupying Germans, she has also the chic, lively 'on the spot' manner of a successful New York or Bostonian editress of a woman's magazine. Sark alone of the islands has put all its eggs in one basket and a very strong basket it appears to be. It is hard to imagine that in the foreseeable future visitors from city life will not be enchanted by an island that carefully advertises its remoteness from the present age. I can think of only one difficulty for Sark – who will succeed the present Dame? He or she will have a hard job to live up to this lady of the old school with a very sure grasp of the realities and opportunities of the modern world.

I came to Alderney in a day of violent wind and rain; and this was quite right too. I have no doubt that this long, rocky, flat-looking island has its calm, sunlit moods, but, in its geographical remoteness from the rest of the group and in its comparatively large areas of treeless heathland, it seems as romantically savage as Sark is pastoral and gentle. Life here must surely always have been very hard and one can easily picture the grim horrors of war-time when Russian prisoners worked there in isolated slavery, cutting fortifications from the rock with their bare hands and dying in hundreds from exhaustion and hunger. Alderney alone of the islands evacu-ated its whole population during the war and it has not, I think, been easy to bring life back to this gaunt world where the grim early-nineteenth-century barracks suggest smuggling and 'the menace of the French' and old Boney. At the centre of this grim world, it is true, lies the charming little town of St Anne with much Regency elegance. Nevertheless only the tourist who wants it primitive would come here. I could visualize the summer visitors in their absence – those now rather dated English middle-class families, father and son in too-long khaki shorts, father rather dictatorial, climbing rocks whose steep-ness puts him a little more out of breath than he wishes to show, mother, blonde and freckled, hardy in any emergency whether it be in the boat or with an outdoor fire, daughter long-legged in too-long grey flannel shorts. Or have such families now vanished from the earth? Even residents must put 'peace and quiet' and cheapness above every other need. Most of the houses are stout fishermen's cottages, life is 'primitive'. A place for some kind of writers – T. H. White, Michael Packe and others – some kind of painters, and retired colonels still agile enough to mess about in boats. A place too with plenty of cheap booze and a first-rate library for the long damp winter evenings. Tourists and residents, however, are not enough to solve the small island's economic problem. There will never be a garrison again; fisheries nowadays are an organized enterprise on a scale beyond Alderney's powers; the slate quarries continue but on too limited a scale. The President of the Island, Commander Herivel, is a remarkable man, a 'character', a rolling stone who has come to rest after many Somerset Maugham adventures; but his rolling has given him great ingenuity. It is he who has brought to Alderney such unexpected light industries as the making of silencers for motor cars and the tinning of ox-tongues from the USA intended for the English market. To carry on this strangely routed meat packing six hundred workers have been brought from poverty-stricken Calabria. To such Alice Through the Looking Glass devices do labour costs bring industry in the modern world. Even with such ingenuity Alderney is not emancipated from the financial tutelage of Guernsey under which she was placed by the British Government after the war. It is difficult to see the future of an island like Alderney. Even in our advanced stage of civilization the number of super-civilized who want to live a rough, primitive life is limited. Far more isolated than Sark geographically, Alderney has nevertheless not been able to establish itself as an 'away from it all' day trip – to arrive by air for the day, apart from the expense, somehow destroys the 'back into the past' atmosphere, and then there are motor cars, though not many, to be seen on Alderney. Yet unless the primitive life on this very romantically savage island is to become too primitive even for the taste of those who have chosen to live there, they must find some tourism or industry sufficient to provide them with the social services and amenities that even 'simple livers' demand today.

*

It is not, however, in the sweetnesses of Sark or the rigours of Alderney that the interesting patterns of Channel Isle life are to be found. Anyone who has landed in Guernsey will remember the acres and acres of glasshouses over which the plane seems to twist and turn. To drive around the coast of Guernsey at once suggests a vital division of interests. Seaward the scene is as imposing and grand as any in Cornwall or Brittany, but only look to the other side of the road and you see acres of ugly bungalows of various unfortunate periods, glasshouses and between each nursery small spaces of ugly scrubland. To repair the schizophrenia that must affect all but the most unseeing of sightseers, I suggested that at least the scrubland might be planted with trees, conifers or, to add to that subtropical appeal of the Island, eucalyptus or palm trees; then those whose eyes strayed for a moment from the sea would not be brought down to earth with too harsh a bump. I met a few residents who did not agree, except the tomato and flower growers. Tree roots, it seemed clear, would interfere with the necessary drainage of the glasshouses. In this simple divergence can be seen the conflict between the agricultural and the tourist interests of the island.

It has been Guernsey's misfortune to lack the same protection from winds as the more southerly Jersey; to grow for the English spring and winter markets can only be done under glass. From small nineteenth-century beginnings with melons and grapes, this has now developed to an industry of tomatoes, spring flowers and chrysanthemums which covers all but a fraction of the countryside. What remains suggests that it was of great beauty – a softer more delicate South Western Ireland. It is hard to imagine a more unfortunate agriculture for an island wishing to appeal to tourists, yet the coast is full enough of little bays and coves and nooks to draw an increasing number of family parties who want quiet holidays.

Jersey from the air has an equally revealing but totally contrasting appearance. A more rolling landscape bathed by a softer wind; early crops are grown outdoors. Some fairly large estates with seventeenth-century stone houses (most of them unfortunately disfigured by prosperous Victorian owners) house the last of the old Jersey seigniorial families, many of them no longer office holders, devoted to charitable works, sailing and sub-tropical gardening. Here also the farms are on a larger scale and stockbreeding still persists though decliningly. The young farmers I met seemed grander, more disposed to motoring abroad and visits to London shows than the tomato growers of Guernsey, though not necessarily for this more prosperous. This richer, fuller, countryside, where palm trees even on a wintry day seem less out of place, has not only land to provide for the luxury resident but also room to expand its tourist trade to meet wholesale demands. So far it has withstood Butlin's but allows one or two locally-organized holiday camps. The glorious Atlantic surfing beaches appeared to be as beautiful as South Africa or the California coast, but I am prepared to believe the residents' complaints that they are less attractive when thousands cover their sands. More accommodating residents, however, suggested that two lady secretaries in bikinis driving a hired car is enough to make many of the retired type of residents speak of Blackpool. The trouble with St Helier, I thought, was that it has none of the glamour of Blackpool nor of the gaiety of Brighton. It is merely a once pretty early-Victorian town that has grown to meet a holiday trade that has added close on one hundred thousand more visitors each year for some years. The shops are good, but on wet days there is little to do but shop, and all residents complained of the horrors of summer shopping. Amusingly enough in order to avoid the crowds these defenders of the English way of life are being driven to resort to American-style drive-in multiple stores built near the airport for the convenience of air crews. The main parade by the harbour is given up to the offices of shipping firms or to some of the hundreds of mushroom car-hire firms which seem to be the main 'up to date' provision Jersey makes for visitors. However, the beaches and hotels outside St Helier are of an exceedingly high standard and no doubt the visitors get all their Blackpool at their own hotel. Anyway, what young holidaymaker now wants what Blackpool used to offer when he or she can get surf-riding, sunbathing, 'Continental style' food and a good dance floor? An elderly taxi driver complained to me that the new visitors can't amuse themselves. 'They want spoon feeding,' he said, 'everything done for them. In the old days the crowds used to form a crocodile back to their houses, singing "One, two, three, four, where are we heading for?" and then cry, "Rosehurst", or "Homeleigh", or whatever the name of the place was. Ah, they knew how to amuse themselves then.' Of course, he was entirely wrong, it was those crocodiles who would roam the streets aimlessly on a wet day not the more sophisticated tripper of today.

Where Jersey has gone out for mass holiday provision, Guernsey has gone out for the 'quieter', more 'old-fashioned' visitor. As a happy result it has in St Peter Port, the capital, one of the prettiest small seaside towns that I know. Rising tiered upon a hill, facing a harbour with a dramatic medieval castle, the town looks out upon all the other islands and further to the coast of Normandy. It is indeed a miniature Regency Naples, with Sark and Jersey its Capri and Ischia. The somewhat sad-looking shops reminded me inevitably of my childhood – is it the window dressing or the shopfronts or the signwriting that is somehow dated? Nothing can give one a more vivid understanding of how the nineteen twenties and even 'thirties, despite their declared emancipation, were still strongly tinged with Victorian colouring than such shopping streets. The tomato growers who buy there, however, live in their present prosperity in a later world of 'contemporary' furnishing, uncut moquette and cocktail cabinets. Perhaps the shops are more suited to the quiet retired residents of the services and colonial pensions kind. Guernsey is a favourite target of breaking-up White Africa, for it is neither so noisy nor so expensive as Jersey – 'more select' this is usually called. The submergence in the inter-war years of the Guernsey countryside under glasshouses has left few of even such moderate-sized manorial properties as are to be seen in Jersey. The growing prosperity of the nurseries has put a very high value on land, and even some restriction on purchasers from outside. But these restrictions relating to rateable value, like all such restrictive legislation, do not appear to be effective. There is a constant stream of buyers from England. An old English garrison centre at Fort George has been demolished and is being replaced by luxury dwellings. The hotel where I stayed bustled with English businessmen and their wives consulting with estate agents and builders. One gentleman, indeed, was so wedded to the City that he carried a transistor to the cocktail bar especially to listen to the stock-market prices. Guernsey, in fact, is now beginning to receive the very rich type of immigrant as well as retired professional people. Their number, one would think, must be strictly limited, for however luxurious the new houses may be, the land available hardly allows for more than an acre of ground to each house. To pay luxury prices – in the ten to twenty thousand pounds range – for such limited accommodation seems at first a considerable sacrifice, but the reward in increased income and in advantage to one's heirs is so great that it apparently seems worth paying. In any case, apart from a few large properties, the very rich immigrants to Jersey, where land is far more easily found, also frequently live in panorama-sited luxury housing estates. Indeed one should think of the Channel Islands' very rich big business fringe as living not in the equivalents of country houses in Wiltshire, or even large near-suburban properties of the Sunningdale or Ashdown Forest type, but rather in the sort of large, luxurious house with small town garden that, death duties allowing, they would otherwise have occupied in Bishop's Avenue or Abbey Road. Jersey, and, to a lesser extent Guernsey, are their London homes, from which some will commute fairly regularly by aeroplane, from which their wives will fly over to shop at Fortnum's and get their hair done at Antoine's. For the equivalent of their country house these self-exiled rich have, after all, the Barbados.

If Guernsey can never hope to compete with Jersey in

accommodating the very rich English, who are so valuable to a small island's revenue, a glance at the brass plaques on the lintels of many elegant Regency doorways shows that the registration of companies is well advanced; though once again Jersey leads with a whole street given up to lawyers and chartered accountants concerned with the complications of British or American income tax law.

It is not only free enterprise's protest against state economy that attaches Jersey and Guernsey to modern England. By a paradox the agricultural and distributive workers in these islands increasingly demand the advantages of a welfare society if they are not to sell their labour on the mainland. It is also true to say that the governments of the two main islands have passed from the old feudal landlords, however much the machinery of government and law may retain its old feudal forms, into the hands of the business class who provide for the lucrative tourist industry and into the hands of up-to-date farmers. These go-ahead men are concerned up to a point with providing education and other social benefits that will equip the island's working force for modern competition. Education is reasonably well advanced in both islands, social security in Guernsey is still a good deal an affair of private charity, but in Jersey the States have reached a point where a national health system is in preparation. All this represents a sort of Asquithian, far-sighted businessman's level of social legislation. But these services are manned largely with people trained in Welfare England. Talking to librarians, education officers, probation officers, psychiatric social workers, national school teachers, medical officers of health, I do not think that they will rest content with services that lag behind English standards. Nor is it likely that the working population will demand less, although apart from the Transport and General Workers' Union there is no marked Trade Union activity nor, of course, any but minor light industries. Nevertheless, the demand for fuller social services will come, and, to a large extent, the tourist industry's needs support this demand. Yet undoubtedly, it could only be met by higher taxation and this in its turn would kill the influx of profitable, tax-paying, land-buying immigrants. Once again material interests conflict.

But all such conflicts are still only latent. It is the farmers, never before so prosperous, both in Jersey and Guernsey, who are openly apprehensive of the future. Already competition from Israel, the Canary Islands and Spain endangers the winter vegetable and fruit market, Holland the flowers and bulbs. Older flower growers in Guernsey told me that they could not compete with low Dutch wages; but it is obvious that what they are not yet competing with is up-to-date methods. The younger farmers are fully aware of this and have little use for talk of special Channel Island traditions of farming or of green fingers. They believe, however, that with adaptation to new methods and with attention to new markets, for example exotic plants, they may well gain by the Common Market with additional European buyers. Certainly airplane services from Jersey to Amsterdam and Paris are paving the way for this.

Nevertheless, there might be an agricultural slump. To the prosperity of Guernsey and Jersey it would not make a great difference. Agriculture contributes only a small percentage of the revenue of either. Nevertheless, it would mean an enormous blow to Channel Island morale. Instead of bringing in 2,500 Breton workers for the potato harvest in Jersey, there would be unemployment in both islands. Apart from the adaptability of the younger farmers themselves, I do not see much that the population could fall back on. There is some electronic work in Guernsey which absorbs surplus labour, but Saint Sampson's, the once flourishing nineteenth-century port for the stone trade, is now only a shell, serving to bring coal for the store houses so that St Peter Port may avoid grime. There would no doubt be an increase in spiv activities to cater for tourists; these were a serious menace immediately after the war, but the influx of doubtful types from the London West End has now been almost eliminated. The car-hire trade appeals most to the less steady youth. The summer hiring pays for one of the few winter amusements open to young people. In both St Helier and St Peter Port on wet Sundays I saw young men driving around the streets or parked waiting to pick up girls. There were not many girls about and they didn't seem very interested. But at least the car costs little – I saw three-year-old Consuls offered at £175 with three years to pay. But the car-hire trade can hardly increase much without total traffic congestion and additions to an already high accident rate.

The hotel business, the chief centre of the tourist industry, employs very few local men. Channel Island men don't care for domestic service work, they feel it to be a loss of status. They scorn waiting and cookery schools. As a result Jersey brings in about six thousand British workers each summer and around three thousand foreigners, mostly Italians from prosperous North Italy. Guernsey, too, employs large numbers of Italians. Only a skeleton staff remains in the winter; many of the Italians serve their winter in the West Indies, so sharing the life of their grandest Channel Island customers. I suspect that, apart from the disinclination of the natives for hotel work, the managers and owners prefer to import seasonally, especially Portuguese, Spanish and Italians who are agreeable to conditions under which Channel Islanders would not live. It is difficult, indeed, at the moment to see what could replace agriculture to absorb local labour.

Would it matter if a great part of the working population of these islands left the island during their working lives? The islands could exist on imported labour for the tourist trade; for the rest they would become a rich man's playground and a retired man's paradise. This sounds all very well. Indeed when I sat in the Guernsey court and realized that most of the Daumier-dressed judges or jurats were ex-colonial administrators able to continue to use their skills, I thought how much better this was than a retirement in England, even granted the possibility of becoming a local JP. The public work that some retired people can do in Guernsey or Jersey really is on a satisfactory level, but it would hardly continue to be so if they

118

became tourist pleasure grounds only. Otherwise the incentives to live there are purely material. None the worse for that if they were not of a special kind. Cost of living there is not cheap for the pensioner, too much food has to be imported, too many tourists put up the prices. No, as one ex-Indian civil servant's wife said to me, 'It is not cheap to live here. But one can entertain.' Once again it seems to me that to be able to entertain is a pleasure of retirement much to be hoped for. Nevertheless the meaning of all this is ultimately cheap drink and cheap cigarettes and nothing to do. I'm not sure that the high rates of lung cancer and sclerosis are important. You've got to die somehow. More serious, I thought, was what two doctors told me – nervous illnesses are very common, perhaps because coming to live on an island in order to live more cheaply is not an adequate reason for living at all.

*

Of course, all this is only an aspect of islands of great beauty, lively and friendly inhabitants where clearly one could live a very delightful life. Nevertheless, somewhere there is a sense of hollowness at the centre. Everything comes from outside and the core of the Channel Islands themselves has been almost eaten away. Pleasant though the old court ceremonies and local customs are, these belong to the world of beefeaters for American tourists or at best to a country gentleman's pastime of folklore. More important is the strange sense that comes to one both in the attractive Regency market of St Peter Port and in St Helier's when one hears country people speaking the patois. Does this really connect with anything French? Once again the ties with the Continent have been gradually loosened. Undoubtedly France's unselfishness helped the Channel Islands greatly during the occupation and to the administrators of that time the link seems vital. But in general of course the British tie was strengthened by the occupation, the connection with Europe got faintly tinged with Nazi doctrine. More importantly the bilingual teaching which is still compulsory in primary and secondary schools is felt by enthusiastic teachers (many of them English, all of them trained in English teachers' colleges) to be a hindrance to the already weighted 11 plus and GCE syllabuses. French speaking, too, because it is connected with the patois is seen as something old-fashioned, uneducated. All the forces of progress are against the European connection. Yet in an infant school in the country in Jersey many children were used to French in the home and in a girls' secondary modern school a whole form of girls of twelve spoke and read French of a very high standard. The tradition is still there. The connection with Caen University remains. More French visitors arrive each year. The Jersey farmers must know French if only to talk to the Breton workers on whom they rely at harvest time. All this, of course, *was* out of date. When the Commonwealth was the only order of the day, then the Channel Islands were a small speck in a far-flung system; they could hope for no more than to scramble for England's crumbs. But if a European order is to come, their position becomes at once more pivotal. Could not the islands find their identity by cultivating the old French connection that seemed finished, acquiring exceptional proficiency in the bilingualism that modern teaching has tended to regard as a waste of time? If, as many Channel Islanders feel, the Islands lack a cultural centre to match their material prosperity, could they not be the centre of the new Anglo-French cultural exchange which must surely come if the Common Market comes? The link is already there. The Channel Islands are unique in having a close relationship with an English and a French University – Exeter and Caen. They also have the geography and the training in hospitality to give the students an ideal life. Why should they not be the scene of the first Anglo-French University?

New and Old on the
Grand Trunk Road
1975

In 1975 I went to India to research for my biography of Rudyard Kipling. I followed his footsteps across North India and Pakistan, where his Indian days were spent. I made general notes on which the following article is based.

                    *
            *   *
                    *

We had almost certainly found it – the house where the monkeys are said to have climbed in at the guest's bedroom window and stolen articles from the dressing table. The guest had been Kipling. I have often thought that these depredations must have stimulated the imaginative growth of the Bandar Log, that wonderfully conceived vituperative symbol for all restless, talkative, self-regarding pseudo-intelligentsias of Western or Westernized society.

The house was clinging, like so much of Simla, to a sheer hillside. A Victorian Englishman's Swiss chalet, with views to match from the fretted verandahs – Annandale Valley a thousand feet below, and the snow-capped Himalayas in the distance. It was beautiful. I should have felt at peace to enjoy it, but the misery of walking between New York skyscrapers or across bridges almost anywhere has taught me that there is no way of being free of vertigo and agoraphobia. The vast heat-laden sky was falling upon me, there appeared to be no foothold on this steep, stony, loose-earthed bank, nothing to save me from falling, no end to a fall from 'The Roof of the World'. I mumbled to my friend Tony that he should go on and photograph the house; I would stay put. Lowering myself, I crouched, eyes closed, in my solitary panic, and tried to give my whole attention to the calming sound of nearby boys playing cricket, and the murmur of their elders playing cards (it was Good Friday, one of a string of religious holidays of all faiths in India's secular State).

Then a boy's voice asked, 'Have you *no* friends, Sir, isn't it?'

The question was probably simple curiosity at my improbable European presence on a hill on the backside of Simla, a town itself now not much visited by foreigners, and anyway, I was in the way of their game. But, as so often in India, it seemed strangely attuned to my inner state. India the mysterious!

*

The bearded young American in the aeroplane from Bombay home said, 'What I was thinking of doing like was that anyone who wanted information like that some of us who have come out can give, should get together, say in New York, but it's got to be something that the initiates can sit down and relate to. There's only one Master. The Master is the Master is the Master. He gave me the most beautiful, loving, sweet advice. He said the first thing you do is to get good understanding on the Path. Right?' And his clean-shaven companion, with heartfelt spiritual enthusiasm, answered, 'Right.'

*

One of the ubiquitous Kims of the Bombay waterfront hauled himself up, dripping, over the embankment wall and then pulled up his shivering sea-soaked monkey on a rope. A bystander gave the boy a banana, half of which he immediately wolfed down in evident feverish hunger, but the other half of which he spared for the equally hungry monkey (a necessary preservation of the tools of one's trade? a peculiar Mowgli-like sympathy between boy and beast? or does love of a pet survive hunger and houselessness?). He strolled over the road and joined two solemn bespectacled elderly gentlemen in dhotis and Gandhi caps who were fascinatedly watching three European shaven-headed youths in white gowns cutting their toe nails with elaborate steel clippers. The pedicure done, the three shaven blonds put forward begging bowls. The elderly gentlemen, in their Hindu piety, placed something in each bowl. The beggar boy stared in admiration at the white

124

professional skill. On this pavement at night sleep hundreds of immigrant villagers who cannot yet find the paise for tents or squatters' shacks. Here in apparently lively, chattering preparation for sleep, they miraculously preserve their family identities as groups, but lose all human shape when asleep, curled up and totally hidden in blanket or sack-like mysterious cocoons.

*

At Delhi airport, waiting for another punctual aeroplane, I sat putting into order my Kipling notes. Or had hoped to if the chatter by my side had not suddenly grown to crowd proportions. On the bench, leaving a decent distance between herself and me, sat a plump, well-shaped middle-aged lady with smiling liquid eyes of extraordinary fascination: sweet marshmallow with an iron will, I sensed, and was reminded of a face I had seen more than once in my Kipling reading, and yet could not exactly recall. Anyway, I was too much fascinated by the knot of her attendants of all ages, children, middle-aged, elderly, even one very old man – between a dozen and twenty of them. Each in turn placed a garland of marigolds and jasmine around her ample shoulders. These she received with sweet smiles and vivacious but soothing chatter. Then each follower in turn prostrated himself or herself flat upon the airport floor and kissed the smiling lady's feet. The last prostrant was a severe humorous-eyed tall lady of seventy or so, like some famous Girton humanist in a sombre sari. I had thought that her grandeur would make her exempt, but in fact her prostration when it came was deeper and the reverent, happy look in her eyes made me ashamed to be watching something so private. As each bowed flat before her, the honoured lady, smiling abstractedly, banged them very hard on the back.

It was foolish of me now, I see, not at once to have guessed what the scene meant. But I didn't and thought of some feudal Rani being seen off by her many attendants and clients. Minutes later in the departure lounge the great lady was left

125

alone with her attentive secretary. She sat back, large, and tired in the midday heat, but with a restful and serene smile. She opened an illustrated magazine, turned the pages rapidly and then sat in contemplation of what she found, with a smile as delighted as that of the ubiquitous Indian children who were everywhere surrounded by their family's total attention. My friend, Tony, acting a quiet detective role, passed behind her, identified the magazine, and, to the surprise of the bookstall seller, bought a copy. It was one of the many English-language women's papers fashioned on *Woman's Own.* Sure enough on one page, the plump, serene face of the important lady smiled back at us, not with her childlike smile of pleasure at seeing her own face, but with her public, restful, placid smile. She had just returned, the article told us, from another successful tour of the States and was about to set up a college of transcendental meditation. Then I remembered who she reminded me of – Madame Blavatsky.

*

The ambiguous Indian sense of spiritual duplicity remains unyieldingly, or rather as always yieldingly but elusively, a mystery. A highly intelligent sophisticated Indian woman novelist in Delhi suggested to me that, perhaps, it was only for export, to help Californian tycoons to avoid thrombosis or to help ageing European hippies to get off the hook. Perhaps she was mocking me – so often the most pleasant encounters with Indian people carry a delicate scent of mockery; but, if she was not, then I think she perhaps had not felt the impact of Hindu worship for a long time.

My own experience of the first impact four years ago of the great Hindu temples of the South, especially of the Shiva puja at the great Temple of Tanjore, of the awe and expectancy that comes with the deafening sounds of the conches and the gongs was in no way diminished when I saw it again in the North. Its surface appearance is so obvious, so crudely theatrical, and then the preparation of awe is pathetically followed by nothing at all.

Kali, if it happens to be one of her temples, is there before the ceremony begins, and she is there again when the music is over, unchanged in her ludicrous primitive horror.

But for me, this tremendous preparation, followed by nothing save the routine clearing away of the ceremonial utensils, of a ceremony that appears hardly to have taken place, produces not disappointment as I have often seen in the faces of expectant Western tourists or the contempt shown by the camera clicks with which the Japanese register this non-event; for me this apparent shapelessness only furthers the dethronement of Reason, or Order, or Personality that the dark, cramped but wonderfully decorated architecture of the temples has begun.

You need (I need) all the deep resources of our inheritance from the last three centuries to resist these ancient (very ancient Shivite) messages of the oneness of destruction and creation, and all the rest of it. Happy Mr Koestler whose Western identity is so firm and resistant. Beside it, the beatifications I once attended in St Peter's seem pure show, and more still the great mosques of Northern India seem empty miracles of architectural beauty. It is easy for Reason and Humanism to survive in such splendidly rational designs, it is hard for them to resist Hindu and Jain worship. Yet to say 'muddle' as E. M. Forster does, even in half praising tones is to register only one's own response, it is to ignore the casual but orderly, gentle but fierce worship that you see.

Something of all this inchoate perplexity must have shown through my attempts to express my enchantment with India in more completely rational terms as I talked with an intelligent young interviewer in Bombay, for he remonstrated sadly, though I had said nothing of the kind, that I seemed to think with Cartier that religion was the key to India. Again, a sensitive young writer, who delighted me by expressing a genuine belief that I had caught important aspects of the sub-continent in *As If By Magic*, said, as if to reassure himself, 'Of course, there is a solid Marxist structure underlying your

analysis,' which, of course, there isn't. It is very understandable this distrust of European fascination with the Hindu
religious scene by all the intelligent and the young and the
active and the sensitive in India. They are angry when someone
comes to India and sees only human excrement and hypocrisy
as V. S. Naipaul did, but they are worried, too, when the
first words spoken in reply to their questions are not the
conventional horror at the poverty of its cities and more still of
its villages, a distaste for the caste system with its mechanical
and often incompetent performance of appropriate tasks
as a daily ritual, its ultimate denial of human dignity in
untouchables and scheduled 'criminal' tribes. Not to begin
with these horrors, no doubt, has echoes for them of the
atrocious parasitism of the Western hippy beggars; it seems to
deny all they are trying to do in making India more decent, a
more concerned, a more free, a more creative, and, a little
more shamefacedly, a more securely defended society. Praise
of the Noh plays produces a similar reaction in young
Japanese.

And threaded through their response is the pervasive sense
that the gap between the words of Ghandi-ji or even Ambedkar,
whose very badly-designed statues abound everywhere, and
the political and social reality of modern India is so great that
foreign praise is either that of a naïve idiot or of someone too
contemptuous to utter the well-worn phrase 'Indian hypocrisy'. In their desire to give their country shape and active
purpose they are constantly weighed down by the contradiction
that this has with the unworkable great ideals from which
modern India sprang. Yet as I tried always to say to them, it is
useless to be stultified by the dead weight of inevitably
compromised ideals. To visit Nehru's house – furnished in the
Healsish style of rich nineteen-thirties progressives with an
appropriate and beautiful Miss Jekyll garden – and to read his
long, well-intentioned but ultimately intensely egoistic message
to the nation about the disposal of his ashes, is to feel all that
embarrassment that comes on an ageing English progressive

like me at the mention of Kingsley Martin's name. Yet it is a useless impeding emotion for me, absurd for the younger generation, and ultimately not really fair to Kingsley Martin or to Nehru. Better to accept the judgement of the Headmaster of Harrow on India's saviour, framed on the wall of the house, which is now a Museum – 'a thoroughly good fellow' – and leave it at that. To accept the hard-won efficiency of his daughter's rule without being blind to its inevitable bullying accompaniment.

*

Let me, then, to make the context clear of my Indophilism, say at once that I shall never forget the first pavement sleepers I saw rolled up like sacks; the professional beggar boy pointing in a mechanical but no less genuine sign to his hungry mouth and rubbing his hunger-swollen stomach; the woman on the steps of Delhi's great mosque holding out two ulcerated stumps in place of arms; the youth in Lahore's bazaar lying on the ground exposing a leprous thigh with a fly-swarmed running sore; perhaps most horrible because most ludicrous and shameful, the shrunken old woman, perhaps ninety but probably sixty, whining mechanically 'No papee, no mamee', the words she must have used since her begging girlhood began. These and a hundred other human horrors, as well as pariah dogs in contorted distress trying to lick the bleeding stumps where their tails were, the sacred cows that have begun to stumble, the thousand flights of a hundred birds, all of them of great beauty and many of great rarity, whose shooting on one day of truce in the momentous head-on collision of Lord Kitchener and Lord Curzon is recorded in stone, all these are horrors. But let me add, not to confuse these two, Dr Johnson's comment that the prospect of being hanged wonderfully concentrates a man's mind. The human suffering to be seen in India does wonders to clear away any confusions one has about the relation of human to animal. It does so by its sheer impact. Its assertion of the superiority of human worth is so strong because it strikes exactly the field of feeling on which the claim for the equality of animals is usually made. Yet the disgrace of animal suffering still remains. And the horror of both is enhanced in India because of the exceptional grace and beauty of any group of villagers by the roadside, or the constantly renewed thrill of the vivid green evening flights of parakeets. And I am not ignorant that the parakeets are on their way to feed upon the crops by which the villagers survive.

Yes, the price of human suffering and endurance because of Indian innerness is high, and it cannot be set off like some Benthamite calculus against her power to survive, to digest successive waves of conquering civilizations – Aryan, Moghul, British. Yet surely the plurality of creeds and customs and costumes and tongues and manners must, at the lowest level, fascinate the Western or Japanese tourist (perhaps it frightens many and disgusts some few). The accretion of religious and cultural expression in great works of architecture and sculpture must touch even the most blind and tour-drunk visitors – Dravidian, Aryan, Moghul, and the fine, yet-to-be-appreciated offerings of the British Raj. Yet I watched again and again groups of *Indian* tourists visiting their ruined cities and palaces and the mosques and temples of faiths that are not their own. They looked and listened to their guides automatically, I thought, as though it was a show that was not their concern. I asked knowledgeable Indian people about what was the average Indian tourist's reaction to his or her land, and was told, and I believe it, that they are mainly saying 'Ah! How rich they must have been then.' Indian people, save for a very few, have *endured* more than they have *done*, so that their history, unless one is to go back into the legendary world of their Gods, is that of their conquerors and not of themselves. Their past, unless it has religious significance, is felt only as an external picture show.

This sense of passivity, of non-participation is perhaps why so many visitors are impressed only by suffering India. I must say that I do not feel like that. I have no doubt of the horrors but

130

I am also struck by the exaggerated effect they have on many visitors, and by the failure of these visitors to feel the vitality of modern India, their failure to offset the deathly side by the variety of the apparent disorder with its intricate patterns of order within, both old patterns and new. The richness that Kipling so wonderfully caught in *Kim.*

Let me first dispose of what is purely touristic about this feast. Something of minor, but not trivial economic importance in the new India. When an Oxford don friend, of sensitivity and intelligence, told me flatly that no tourists should go to India because it is shameful to travel for pleasure among such misery (he was excusing my last trip because of its relation to my work in progress on Kipling, but suggesting, I think, that, after that, enough was enough), my immediate feeling was one of amazement that we should shun the poor and the destitute as though they were not only untouchables to some of their fellow Indians but unseeable to the world at large. Yet the simple practical considerations of the question are as important. Whatever the corruption, and, in a corrupt world, poor countries are expectedly more corrupt than rich ones, some part of India's growing tourist trade must help some of her poor, just as, despite all the novelist's licence of sensibility that I gave myself in my novel, *As If By Magic*, I know that some part of the Green Revolution, despite its many failures, relieves her distress. In return, it should be said, that India's tourist industry offers unique and solid rewards to the visitor. It is one of the best proofs of the Indian power of organization and efficiency and it is right under the noses of the visitors who see only inertia and muddle. The hotels, especially the old-fashioned Raj ones, are a delight to stay in and an unusually spacious delight, so many with magnificent gardens of herbaceous borders and roses (surely a heritage from the Memsahibs rather than the Moghuls). There is friendly concern even from receptionists something almost unknown to me anywhere else in the world. And yet, even in the big modern hotels, the wonderful Indian scene is present. Each hotel has its

131

own tric-tac of daily life among its workers and shopkeepers reproducing all the vitality, langour, gossip and hard bargaining which make up the fascination of the general Indian scene in the streets, the bazaars, and the villages. The food, save for one or two first-rate buffet luncheon counters, is bad when it tries to be Continental, tricky for ageing Western stomachs in its Indian excellence, dull but nostalgic and very well cooked in its faded Raj aspect of tipsycake and bread and butter pudding. Meat and poultry as in most hot countries are scrawny, but, here one meets the New India of efficiency, for everywhere, however far inland, there is delicious and very safe fish to eat. I lived during this last visit mainly on excellent fish and chips. Americans, whom travel reveals in their most depressing insular guise, always refuse fish, but are unable to do without their habitual fresh salads and iced water, sure harbingers of whatever bacteria may threaten the visitor. Yet by far the most 'American' tourists were the Iranian football team at Jallandur who demanded again and again, 'Beefsteaks. Just plain beefsteaks', and, at last, still showing no comprehension of the enormity of their demand, 'OK, give us fried chicken.'

This America-style *naïveté*, so pleasant at home in America, is insupportable abroad. In an hotel where the very elderly waiters with desperate grievances were practising non-cooperation to the extent of wearing armbands saying, 'We want a bonus', most visitors remained ashamedly silent. Only an American lady, peering at the waiter's arm as he served her, told the dining room at large – ' "We want a bonus." Well! I suppose we all want that.'

My sensitive don friend will note only the hypocrisy that I, too, ate and accepted the friendly service where exploitation was rife. True and so it is in all but a handful of places where tourists visit outside the major industrialized countries. Why is it that India must be excepted?

As if all societies were not riddled with such contradictions. Is it only because their vast, over-swollen population makes all these disfigurements loom larger than in other countries? I am

132

not convinced of this. Who that has seen the *bédonville* shanty towns of Paris or the slums of a dozen or so American cities, or of Tokyo, let alone of Naples, can be so insistent on the corrugated iron-roofed shacks of the squatters that line the route from Bombay airport to the city? But visitors to India *are* so insistent.

India, I suspect, has become the whipping boy for all the doubts and anxieties of the materialist, forward-going, out-ward-looking West, as it has become the ludicrous Utopia of their rebellious sons and daughters, the necessary arguing point in a tedious and, for her, largely irrelevant Western generational war. Yet this symbolic, select India seems to have infected many Indians, so that they often do not notice the elements of Western progress in their own society. A man with a special interest in the urban culture of Bombay, claimed that his knowledge of the insufficient public toilet provision was exact, yet we pointed out to his surprise a number of public toilets provided by the municipality where they were most needed, in the shanty towns.

*

The Sikh community is, at once, the best and the worst assertion of India's outgoingness, for they speak for it and yet they seem to suggest that it is the special contribution of their community. Yet among this forward-looking, outgoing group there is a curious halfness. It is true that the public kitchens and dining rooms and the hospital at the Golden Temple in Amritsar immediately proclaim an exceptional element of good works in the Sikh faith among the surrounding religions. Yet it is hard to understand why, if free provision has been so splendidly made for chest X-rays for pilgrims, the X-ray machine should be crowded into cupboard space along with the clerk registrar's desk and typewriter when the grounds of the Temple are so extensive. Muddle in the midst of efficiency.

By contrast, a visit to a Temple of the Jains, those most uncompromisingly spiritual of monastic sects, whose extreme

133

devotees wear mouth masks to prevent the chance inhalation of nearly invisible insects that house souls in their lowly progress on the Wheel, may well confront you with an army of lamps or air conditioners or fans proclaiming their manufacture by one of the large Jain firms. Wealth in the midst of extreme asceticism.

For more uncompromising signs of the outgoingness you have only to go up Kim's Grand Trunk Road beyond Cawnpore to Amristar and on through Pakistan to Peshawar. In one respect Kipling's world has not changed: where military readiness is not the prevailing note, extensive new projects of road or bridge or factory building are in ample evidence. Kipling's two hero types of subaltern and engineer still dominate on both sides of the frontier. That much of this activity is a reminder of the futile wastefulness of Partition is only half the story, though a monstrous one.

I believe that, for Kipling, the Partition would, as it should for anyone, be one of the cruellest horrors of the sub-continent scene. And that, not least, because, instead of the Cossack spies disguised as tourists of the Kipling stories, there are the depressing parties of invited Soviet or Chinese visitors that India and Pakistan feel forced to summon as warning signals to each other.

One such Soviet party I saw in Delhi zoo: they were dressed as always for an English nineteen-thirties coach outing to Blackpool. Sweating and overweight, they passed through, without noticing, a teeming crowd of excited, graceful Indian village children on their first visit to the city. Another group, more scary and science fiction, took over Pindi airport lounge: these were Red Chinese looking like unisex invaders from space in an episode of *Doctor Who*.

Yet, here again, what is one to make of this feverish military and diplomatic scene, where tales of the cruelties and horrors of 1947 come more hysterically and suddenly and truthfully both on Indian and Pakistani social occasions than do any of the gradually vanishing outrages of the Raj? For, when you actually get to the frontier, although non-Indians or Pakistanis cross with you, although you are greeted on both sides by assurances that those chaps over there are busy arming, isn't it, immigration officials and customs men show a quiet courtesy unknown to me at any other frontier; and the No Man's Land, as you walk along an avenue between carefully planted hibiscus bushes, reveals on each side acres of fertile wheatland. To anyone who has seen the Berlin Wall, or the machine-gun towers on the road from Bratislava out of Czechoslovakia to Austria, this peaceful country scene appears to be an extraordinary Indian play acting, but it is play acting that has erupted into savagery as dreadful as, if less calculated than, that along the Iron Curtain.

*

I am drawn to this quality of people to act out themselves. Apart from the natural, human, and aesthetic beauties of the sub-continent, it is a perfect place for a novelist who delights in Dickensian theatre. The motivations for this larger than life quality are many – the need to assert one's very existence in a country so enormously overcrowded, the caste need to act one's part, the needs of minorities – Moslems, Sikhs, Christians, Parsis – to assert themselves, but, on top of all this, I believe, a more modern need of search for identity in an increasingly socially mobile world. How rich this daily intercourse would be if one could speak Hindi, or better still Hindi, and Urdu, and Telegu, or better still many more of the languages, I can only guess at, but it makes me very envious of those who do, for, of course, it is only a tiny fraction of the millions who can produce for you however haltingly their personal dramas, yet if I can judge by the brilliance of the dumb show of others, I am missing the material of a thousand novels.

Of the many encounters I had, absurd, hilarious, pathetic, mysterious, here are a few. I have left telling them to the end, because to tell them before I had said anything about my reactions to India (and Pakistan and Ceylon) would be a churlish return for the pleasure and hospitality I have received. My account would seem frivolous.

Coming back through the crowded Mediterranean evening *passegiata* of trafficless Simla, a middle-aged, shabby but dapper man suddenly introduces himself.

'Sir, I am only a poor government clerk . . .' I make noises to suggest my high regard for clerical aptitude, Tony makes noises to suggest his great respect for government service. I think immediately of Dostoevsky and Chekhov and the ramifications of the Tsarist bureaucracy. The clerk continues, 'I am very interested in the lives of great men. I have written a talk for Radio India on Abraham Lincoln. They reply that it is not to be produced, but I think that this failure will not count against me in the service.' We looked sad and I angry that any recrimination for such artistic failure should be conceivable. He cheers us: 'I intend to give some lectures on the French Revolution, Thomas Carlyle, Young Arthur . . .' (who this is I don't know – King John's nephew? the pretty boy in 'Tom Brown's Schooldays'? Arthur Young, the eighteenth-century agronomist?) . . . 'Abraham Lincoln, William Ewart Gladstone, and other topics. Marat, Sir, was murdered in his bath, Abraham Lincoln in the theatre.' Now he is dramatic: 'The great man is dead. Mrs Gladstone lies upon the grave. "Oh pappie, pappie, don't go from us," she cries.' I expect a denouement of suttee, but perhaps the clerk saw that he was approaching the same unlikely climax, for his tone changes. 'I am glad that I had the courage to speak to you, Sir. Great courage is always desirable, but it is hard.' It is hard, too, as we were finding, to sympathize with such sentiments without appearing condescending. 'Yesterday I had the courage to speak to another couple. Also from the UK.' Save for the touch of Dostoevskyan malice towards us implied, I think, in the revelation of the repertory nature of his role, the 'poor clerk' was not a solely Indian character, or, if so, simply one of the 'hopeless', the 'lost' as much as any beggar, but a debris not of ancient India but of the Raj.

*

136

Another part of the bad heritage was that of the many university lecturers who told me that they were teaching their wretched students Collins and Grey, or of the schoolboys whose 'lessons' were the learning by heart of 'Lucy' and 'The Charge of the Light Brigade'. The Western muddle so marked in many semi-educated Christians like the Catholic gentleman who gave me the history of St Francis Xavier: 'In 1242, Sir, he was a student at the University of Paris. St Augustine had just returned there from the Napoleonic Wars and he told the boy Francis, "How shall it profit a man" – you know the old text, Sir. So the boy Francis set off for Goa.'

*

Identifications are not always so simple. In a hotel I was standing alone in the bar, when a handsome middle-aged woman rushes in, 'Oh, if I had known you were a writer! My God! When I tell my son! He's a good looker and a six-footer too! But books, everything is books for him. All very well. But I must work. I must be housekeeper here in this hotel to keep him at college. How is it by the way, service and so forth? My husband was an officer. My God, what a good looker and a six-footer also. The heart goes one day. He is dead they tell me. So what are you going to do? Pluck and courage and so forth, isn't it? So here I am working. But what can it be? No training. All right. So I make a good housekeeper. Work keeps you young and all that.' At first glance, of course, simply one of the 'plucky' ladies of the nineteen thirties, the butts of my early short stories, but the comparison has little meaning really. I think of the non-existence, the shame of widowhood in India fifty years ago let alone the existence of suttee a hundred years further back. Here, surely, is mobility to demand admiration, the more so when she adds, 'My daughter will not be a housekeeper. "No, Ma," she said, "I must have a career, isn't it?" "Of course, child," I said, "that's how it must be." So she will go to College too.'

Upward mobility can be frustrating, too, in a land largely deprived of imports. A young very elegant Sikh and his beautiful girl friend, plucking as they so often do at her sari in a fussy delicate feminine gesture that does much to impair the universal praise of the beauty of the saris in India, sit down nonchalantly in the lounge of an elegant but rather remote hotel. He snaps his fingers in the air behind in a lordly gesture to an imaginary host of waiters, 'Wine list! Wine list!' The barman detaches himself from behind the bar and advances. 'Do you wish gin, Sir, or whiskey, or beer?' 'I want the wine list.' 'Sir, I can sell you no wine. We have no wine.' 'No, no. I don't want wine. Bring me a whiskey and a fresh lime and soda with ice. But why is there no wine list? This is meant to be a tip top hotel. You tell the manager. He must have a wine list.'

But it is even harder to bear moving down and requires as much histrionics. The elderly guide at the ruined city was once the employee of the Maharani, but now of the equivalent of the Ministry of the Environment. His first remark to me is, 'Don't tell me your nationality, Sir, no, no, I don't want to hear it.' After the question put by passing boys in the street that occurs three or four times a day – 'From which country do you come, Sir?' – I am rather relieved. But we have not gone far with the history of the city, when he cries again, 'I must not know your nationality, no, no. That is not my business. That is waste of time. That is not culture.' Feeling some frustration in his return to the subject, I say that I am from the UK. 'No, no, Sir. I don't hear it. It is not my concern. The Maharani has said, the tourists are our friends, ask them where they come from, be interested in their lives. But the gentlemen from Delhi say, Oh no, no, you are not paid for that. You waste the visitors' time. So I don't hear what you say. That is not my affair.' Then, showing me his thread, 'I am a Brahmin, Sir. Not now. Now I am an Indian citizen. No, no, you have not met a Brahmin. That will only waste your time.'

Sometimes changing India can drive the less secure to

extremes of despair. The man at Jaipur was young, a little educated, not prosperous. To me suddenly from a bench: 'Sir, my brain is on fire against all these women. Many are forty years old and not married. But this women's rights makes everything possible for them. They should be taxed double, treble. Everything should be taken from them.' His excitement abated, he speaks as the rational considering man of good sense, 'A man is an inventive animal. He earns 10,000 rupees, now 12,000, now perhaps twenty, in time God knows what. The woman can be proud to be married to such a man, isn't it? Women's rights! My God!'

After showing me some nineteenth-century memorial tablets, a lay curator of Allahabad Anglican Cathedral gave me warning of the UK's decline: 'The English have lost their greatness first in luxury, then in laziness. But still they are more civilized than the Americans. In America all is materialism and politics.' I disagreed. 'I suppose in some parts or in some circles that might be so.' 'No, no. Not might be. I don't allow might be. I am a Christian. When I say so, it is so.'

But in general the treatment of the stranger is not so aggressive – it is more teasing, more humorous, more aware of his stock responses and ready to play with them.

The Maharajah knows very well the reputation of his rank for eccentricity, he knows, too, the decline in his position. The only guests that night in his hotel, Tony and I are invited to dine with him in his palace. When he learns that I am to visit Simla, he calls his Secretary to get 'the Chief Minister of Himachal Pradesh [Simla is the capital of HP province], immediate!' on the telephone, adding, 'and get me Delhi, immediate, and Washington, immediate.' Through to the Minister's secretary he explains that, staying at his hotel, is a professor who, on arrival at Simla, must be given special attention. 'He is rather old and probably bogus. And at the moment his face is covered in mango.' All this is said without a trace of a smile. As the dinner, an amusing lively meal, proceeds, he fears, I think, that we are disappointed, for when I turn to speak to him I see, not his handsome military features, but the soles of two brown feet and a voice from the floor asks, 'How long since you chaps saw a man standing on his head?' He then gets up and does a brief sword dance. Beginning to doubt that we could keep up our end of this histrionic act, I decided to pay some compliment on the furnishings of the long dining-room as a means of hastening towards the end of the entertainment, but my carefully acquired good taste leads me to reject the ancestral portraits, the imposing furniture, and light at last on a simple, well-made cane basket. 'What wonderful workmanship.' The Maharajah is delighted. 'Oh, I am so glad you like it. It is my laundry basket.' He takes out in turn two or three garments. 'Look! the shirt I wore today. The pants. Oh yes, we want you to see everything.' Ghastly good taste lost me that round.

*

A German lady hopes that the two waiters at the Government Hotel are married men and that, if so, they practise family planning. 'Yes, I am a family planning man,' says the young one. 'How many children do you have?' 'Eleven,' he replies. She looks amazed, but turns to the other waiter. 'And you?' 'Eleven also,' the young one replies for him. 'He has eleven girls, and I have eleven boys.' Then the elder man tells her, 'Oh, yes. It will be most profitable for us. There will be a very good football game. My girls against his boys.' Collapse of impertinent stout German lady. But the joke not only rebukes the impertinence, but beautifully reflects Indian family planning problems, where birth control is too often avoided because it throws traditional filial support in old age into jeopardy.

*

Going out of Peshawar, in another direction to the Khyber, is the fine Kohat pass where Kipling's tipsy drummer boys performed their ambiguous heroics in 'The Drums of Fore and

After'. Returning from there we pass through a tribal village. Here cottage gunmaking is Pakistan's solution to rural poverty and tribal unrest. The driver, as usual, has a relation who will gladly offer us mint tea. As usual, also, the relation is anxious to sell to me – guns of every description. British First World War, French colonial, American Second World War, pistols disguised as fountain pens, Japanese stens, all are hand-made in his backyard factory. But I don't want any arms. Anyway, I am reminded of the dangers of air hijacking, and wonder at the ease of these sales to tourists, however usefully the manufactures may help to occupy this restless tribe. Disgusted at last by his failure to make a sale to me, our host says, 'I am disappointed in you. Yesterday we have a visitor from France, a lady, a little older than you, I think, eighty-five years or more. She bought three hundred guns to take away. And you, a gentleman, isn't it? buy nothing!' It was a use for the 'isn't it' which I had heard so often that I had not expected.

However, searches are made. Again and again our luggage is examined, and we are frisked by solemn officials. I wonder where the French lady put her guns? One day Tony is being searched by a tall, fierce and impressive looking Sikh. 'Arms up, please. Now, down.' Feeling in his breast pocket, sternly, 'What's this, Sir?' Then pulling out a comb, he breaks into giggles and combs Tony's hair for him.

Or then again your joke may be taken up by an Indian friend and gently but firmly put in its place. We were going round the Bombay Zoo with a young film actor. He takes us to see the jumbled ranks of discarded Raj statues, standing in a rough line, grave mid-Victorian statesmen and soldiers, some without arms, others without a head. Here indeed is the British Empire made one with Tyre and Nineveh. At the centre sits Queen Victoria, noseless on her throne. I was upset, I suppose, that it all meant so little, so soon, and joked: 'How careless of the Queen to lose her nose,' I say. 'She was more careful of her crown.' Our friend smiles politely, but he answers, 'I hope that this statue will not be here if your Queen is visiting. I know how greatly the English admire us Indians for our family piety.'

*

But in the end I come back to Indian ambiguity. Young Mr K. is writing about my work. We have met and have quickly found it possible to talk with full and pleasant understanding of each other. I invite him to dine with me. We are sitting alone in the lounge before dinner, when a young man enters and sits a little distance away, observing our every movement. It is distracting. I suggest that we go into dinner. As we pass the young man, he rises, and bows. Mr K. introduces him: 'My pupil, Mr Y. This is a great honour for him.' Mr Y. says eagerly, 'I listen to every word. It is wonderful.' I ask him how he enjoys studying English under Mr K., but he appears not to understand. 'Poor Mr Y. He understands little English,' Mr K. says. With difficulty I accept this and we walk on. Out from an alcove comes a middle-aged lady, smiling. 'This is Mr Y.'s mother,' says Mr K. I smile and bow, and, bewildered, ask, 'Do you live far from here?' No reply. 'My Mother speaks no English, Sir, I am afraid,' says Mr Y. with perfect ease of colloquial English. They leave. When we have ordered dinner, I ask Mr K. what it has all been about. He smiles mysteriously. 'We are all so happy to see you in India.' I realize that I am to say no more. Certainly India is the only country I can think of where I could be so happy that I don't mind being told to keep my mouth shut.

Martinique
1980

*
   *   *
   *

After finishing a Fall semester's teaching in America I thought of Europe, I thought of France. And so I went to New Orleans: a remarkable survival of France in America, but really only like itself. The food was good and French, though I can't say I like not being able to make a table reservation, and being expected to stand in line – IN THE STREET – in a nippy wind. At one restaurant an American handed me his coat and said, in the old British colonial way, 'Take that, my man.' I replied in shrill echoes of Gilbert and Sullivan, 'Sir, I am a visiting Englishman, and very bad manners you have.' Perhaps it was this incident (very unusual in my experience of the US), and the bitter reminder of British defeat at Chalmette nearby that made me fly to Martinique.

*

Yes, this was tropical France, and it lived up to my expectations in every way. I was drawn not only by France, but out of curiosity, for this was the family homeland of Wolcott Balestier, friend of Henry James and brother of Caroline, who married Kipling. And, of added interest, Martinique was the birthplace of the Empress Josephine and Madame de Maintenon.

At noon in a small village in the interior, with vaguely Normandy French buildings, a crocodile of small children in white pinafores left their school singing the Marseillaise, and some young men under a faded sign, 'God Bless America',

145

played boules, the southern French outdoor bowls. The same village had a memorial to a citizen who had been responsible for abolishing slavery on the island; his statue proudly carried the text that no French territory had slaves. This unrhetorical French rationalism was carried further in the title of the public rest room: *Chalet de Necessité.*

Fort de France, the capital, has a very fine central square, a park in fact, with palm trees and flowering shrubs, and the whole surrounded by romantic fretworked public buildings. There is a good statue of the Empress Josephine, whose fascinating birthplace lies a few miles away in the lovely rolling landscape of Martinique. I ended one tour of the island at an excellent fish restaurant in St Pierre, near Mont Pelée, which dominates the town. The volcano erupted with terrifying ferocity in May 1902, when an estimated 40,000 people died. So far as is known, only thirty people were believed to have survived of all those who were in St Pierre at the time. A pathetic reminder of the glory that was St Pierre are the double staircase steps of the former opera house: they now lead into a field. It was difficult to credit that peaceful-looking mountain, picturesquely resting in the noonday sun, with such devastating violence as I watched two lizards making love under a hibiscus.

*

The off-season calm and pleasure I found in Martinique was certainly not in evidence when I visited the island again at Christmas one year: the airport had been expanded and jumbo jets from France, the USA and Canada arrived by the minute, swamping the island with sun seekers. The island sank visibly. I escaped to Robert, a small seaside resort on the far side. All was quiet as I sat reading on the waterfront, until I became aware of two armed policeman watching me with suspicion. Then crowds began to gather, like rain clouds in the clear blue sky, and on a balcony appeared President Giscard to address the French people. There was no peace there or elsewhere on the island, which, like all islands, should be avoided in the take-your-clothes-off season. An American visitor at the hotel said very typically, 'I don't pretend to care for the French very much, but in these days it does to be in French territory. For French countries are always a symbol of law and order.' The next day we went into Fort de France, and saw the severe damage caused to the Palais de Justice by nationalistic rebels, by a bomb during the night.

America – a Celebration
1980

This little piece was written in the United States. As my many visits to America inevitably suggest an end to that connection, I grow more thankful to the universities whose invitations have enriched my middle and late years so enormously.

*
*   *
*

I first came to the United States in 1960, when I was already 47. My picture of the new land I had entered was formed from John Dos Passos's novels (much too underrated now), 1930s movies seen again and again, often three times in one sitting, and the popular tunes of the 1920s and 1930s which still come into my head when Chatanooga or Basin Street or Omaha or a hundred other places in the United States are mentioned.

It's hard sometimes nowadays to know whether Georgia is on my mind because I love that beautiful state or because the song haunted my happy undergraduate days at Oxford.

For various reasons, when I landed at Los Angeles Airport in 1960, I came as someone temporarily very tired of England, even of Europe, so – never mind the smog, never mind the freeways (as a matter of fact, I'm addicted to freeways), never mind the police car stopping suspiciously when you do that mad English thing of walking a few blocks – I have held to my love of LA ever since.

That's not a popular thing to show on the Atlantic side of the USA, as I learned when I got to New York. 'I love Los Angeles,' I say.

'You mean San Francisco,' they answer.

'No.'

'But all Europeans love San Francisco.'

'Yes, but I love Los Angeles.'

And I mean it.

151

The wonderful thing, of course, on that first visit was the lack of class consciousness, still, alas, a factor in England.

I found it all over the states as I visited and lectured in the Midwest and New England and, yes, wait for it, in the South (with some exceptions). No snobbery and immediate friendliness and courtesy which breaks down all barriers of reserve.

Of course, I know that in some US circles wealth takes on a majesty that can put our dukes to shame. And there are grand families, though I've not often been invited to society hill in America. But my experience has been of a snob-free air right across the states and that's quite something to say for a continent.

Of course, there are pervasive American attitudes I find it difficult to take. I had a basinful of sport-worship in boyhood from my father. Now I dread the very sound of the marching band rehearsing for the game – there is so much high-powered energy. But then this high energy of leisure time and special occasions is, I suppose, the reverse side of the work ethic which dominates so much thinking across the United States. If work is to rule your life, you need to get all you can out of play – trick or treat; tuxedos and ballroom gowns for the high school graduation dinner at the local Holiday Inn; and so on through life in an all-pervasive fever.

I was hit by the work ethic three years back; a woman once regretted to me that her son with an asthma allergy had gone to Arizona.

'But the dry desert air will cure it,' I suggested.

She smiled sadly at my easy hedonism.

'If a man loses his allergy, he loses his will to work, Angus.'

Well, Maggie Thatcher's trying to teach us the work ethic in England. But I've always worked hard and been a pleasure lover.

I suppose I connect this work-worship I only half admire with the survival of the frontier myth that makes even small boys of eight walk with a macho roll and sets stickers on cars saying, 'If a man doesn't carry a gun, he isn't a man.' It makes me shiver, but then I think of the courteous and cool driving within a 55-mile limit on US highways. I compare it with Italian or English or French driving, and Germans driving on their autobahns at 90 and more miles an hour – a fast, dangerous and aggressive let-up from work tension.

But men are still men in other ways in America: near the home of the great US architect, Frank Lloyd Wright, I was looking at some photos of Wright in a restaurant, when a local man said, 'I'll tell you two things about Lloyd Wright – one, he messed about with women, but that doesn't matter; two, he didn't pay his debts, and, sir, that does matter.'

But my impression is that the position of women is improving rapidly all the time – not with the shrillness of women's lib's early days, but naturally and easily – with only a few sad cases I can see among intelligent women in their 50s for whom the new life has come too late.

That's one of the changes I have seen that I like. And the rehabilitation of downtowns, the making of fine 1850s factories into elegant malls with first-rate restaurants and outdoor cafés. Surely America owes some of this to the now unmentionable generation of the late 1960s who travelled and were not ashamed to bring foreign ways back to the United States and adapt them.

Another is the emergence of a whole senior citizen world which you see in cafés and restaurants at lunchtime enjoying themselves in an easy mixture of men and women who seem in retirement to have shed both any qualms about relaxation and segregation of the sexes.

I wish our little groups of old male grumblers in the pubs or old ladies gossiping over tea could take life as easily and together. However, 60-year-old ladies in England are beginning to wear pants; perhaps, when, as here, 80-year-olds appear in jeans, we shall have the same easy spirit.

But maybe such differences are only right in a world of variety. I cannot see Europe ever again having the regular churchgoing I see all over the United States, nor England the intense family life – for that you have to go to the United States and to France. (I hardly dare to put the two names together in this country.)

However, setting my grumbles and observations on one side, when I think of the warmth and generosity of the people, the beauty and variety of the scenery and architecture of this vast land, I am proud to remember that in the Fort McHenry Visitors' Center, I stood to attention with my eyes wet, when, as the automatic curtain slid back to the strains of *The Star Spangled Banner*, I saw the American flag flying in the breeze over the Fort. And the British were defeated!

But then, on my first visit in 1960, I was paid a very high compliment: my hair was already white and rather long. I was sitting in a restaurant in New York State, when a small boy of five at the next table who had been staring at me said, 'Mommy, is that George Washington?'

'No dear, of course not; ssh!'

'Well it looks like George Washington.'

However, earlier this year I thought I should get another haircut. An eccentric old lady stopped me in a Minneapolis park and said, 'You look like Einstein. May I stroke your hair?'

But I shall always remember the Washington compliment. I feel that I fitted in from the start. Except for my English accent.

Only last week I asked at a bar, 'Do you have a Pernod here?'

The waitress said, 'A piano? No. Do you want a drink?'

Stupid to have asked for a French drink, of course.

Anyway, thanks America. Take care.

Sri Lankan Journal
1978

```
        *
    *       *
        *
```

What is your name? What is your name?
The chappering children scream.
But 'Wilson' does not satisfy:
Impatiently they cry,
What does it mean? What does it mean?

The thought of Christmas jollities in England, as always, depresses me, but the expectation of a second visit to Ceylon helps to banish gloomy thoughts. Tiredness after a Fall semester teaching in America; worry about whether I had made the right decision not to accept a full-time teaching post there, all add to depression. Even the pleasure of an Indian friend's first visit to England could not wholly lift the lid. But above all, irritation at not being able to get on with the novel which had come to me nearly a year before at Aranjuez. By the time I set off for Delaware at the end of August I had all the shaping and research done. But in Newark I got no more than 10,000 words written. Now we are off to Ceylon, decisions made and uninterrupted time to write lies ahead.

*

MASS TRAVEL IS GOOD – if there were a Maoist regime in England I should have to parade for years with that poster round my neck before I was indoctrinated enough.

*

157

From the airport by taxi to rooms in a Colombo private house, we are immediately far away from tourism. Just before sunset, crows coming from behind the house to roost in the trees of the park opposite, flying into the sunset. They take about one hour to settle down, moving from tree to tree, cawing and squabbling like an outing of old age pensioners. Then, from behind the roosting trees of the crows, from other trees further off, nearer the dying sun, flying foxes begin to leave *their* roosts and gradually fly eastwards to their feeding grounds. A slow ungainly flapping flight, some of the females have babies hanging to their breasts. Against the sunset they look like pieces of charred paper blown up from the heat of a great bonfire.

*

The nurse, who has left her duties to wait on us, says, 'we hate crows'. Her doctor employer (our landlord) confirms this: 'They bring Newcastle disease.' The nurse leaves her children with grandmother for two or three years near Kandy, and will go by herself for a job in the UK. Yet her husband is a sergeant and they have a non. comm. apartment. It is more in reverse than Alice Kipling who lived in the old Raj. She sent her *children* away.

*

The Minah is 'number 2 bird in Sri Lanka'.

*

Our landlady is accompanied by her husband on business or shopping trips; she drives, or the chauffeur. Always beautifully tea-gowned as she emerges from the great elegance of the house. Like an early Fabian hostess.

*

In the park: 'What is your name? What is your country? What is your hotel?' Once this staccato and severe catechism is answered, all is jolly and delighted interest.

*

On the way to a friend's house, the red number plate of Tony's self-drive car deceived a wayside man with a small girl. He hailed T. to stop, and then piled in. 'Just one half-mile please. This girl is very tired.' T. agreed. Then halfway down the lane the man cried out, 'Oh, my God! You are not a taxi. How can I ever repay your kindness. Oh, the insult!'

*

I begin to worry about the car being okay, about water purification, the road, stomach pains, the novel and my future. No satisfying answer to any of them, only the short mocking laugh of the geckos on the walls as they peer at me over the picture frames.

*

In the park, a student: 'What is your country? How old are you? Are you married? I have a German friend. Your watch is very feeble. My German friend has a fine watch. You must learn these words – *Paye* is cock, *Hutte* is fuck. What is fucking between the legs called? Is your cock big, sir? My cock is very small. How do you call it when the cock rises?'

*

At the seashore house into which we have moved, Robert, who looks after us, is wonderfully attentive. But dinner is late. He has an alarm given to him by a Swiss lady, but won't use it in case the noise should disturb us. I point out that I could not possibly hear it from the kitchen, and anyway I am wearing ear plugs when working. He repeats, 'ear plugs'. 'Yes, sir, I do everything to make you happy.' I have to leave him *my* watch every day.

*

A foreign resident, who is constantly pouring oil on troubled Sri Lankan waters, praises the national medical service, but a Singhalese friend says, 'Nonsense. It is very bad, and the hospitals are dirty.' However, as I remember from my first visit, Lady Wilberforce's life was saved in Kandy hospital after she had been butted by an elephant. And only the day before an hysterical mother with a vomiting child was able to get to the village dispensary where the doctor helps. It is open from 8 to 12 every day, and the doctor can be reached at his private house at any other time.

*

Boy in Zoo: 'What is your country?', then, not waiting for an answer, 'Take my photo!'

*

Young employee of the travel agent wants to know why T. is bothering with Jaffna, as equally was a man who stopped his car as we walked in the village: 'You must go south, that is much better.'

*

Survival of old English phrases: a retired banker in the village, 'You see, I was a bad egg, so my parents sent me to Jaffna college'; 'I like the village here, but this house I have at present is not my cup of tea.'

*

Small crabs always on house terrace. Robert feeds them with rice.

*

On the balcony where I am writing, looking out over the pool and garden to the sea, my world is part of that of ants and spiders.

*

Robert tells me that the previous owner (who built the house) had to leave Colombo (some ten miles away) because of the noise when he purchased a new deaf aid.

*

Robert speaks much of Our Lord: 'Our Lord always did this or that.' I am puzzled as he is a Buddhist. Probably he means the Lord Buddha. 'I cured Our Lord of diarrhoea by giving him burnt toast; and then I cured his cold by making him inhale the fumes of coriander seed.' It was then clear that he was referring to a previous tenant, Lord Maugham.

*

A beach walk. 'You want to see cobra, sir?' No thanks. Then surrounded by twenty-eight small children and one puppy, all chappering at once. A slightly older girl with a broom, giggling as she swings it violently over her head. She reduces all the other children to rolling-about fits of laughter with her imitation of my voice.

*

In the Tourist Hotel, Edwardian tea-room pieces played by a group: six violins, one piano, one viola. No musack. Imposing advertisement for an evening entertainment: 'Gully Gully Man, 9.30 p.m., snake-charmer, grows mango tree in two minutes out of seeds, fire-eater and etc., 15 rupees.'

*

A man in the street: 'How is England, sir? Very bad race relations, I hear.'

*

Sunday at the Tourist Hotel. A young receptionist at the bar with his friends, laughing and talking. English manager admonishes him and sends him about his business. The young receptionist, grumbling, goes away muttering, 'These are my friends.' Is this Singhalese umbrage? Or is it just youth? Here

161

is a novelist's dilemma: did I once know more surely or did I presume more easily?

*

Monday, Poya day: I am cold at night owing to the air conditioner – I don't know how to turn it off. I wear a sweater and over that my overcoat for breakfast. Robert can't stop laughing. Later he brings his granddaughter, then her parents. Very elegant. Crow pecking at swollen dead fish on beach. Interruption of my novel by scarlet woodpecker.

*

Schwitzerdeutsch at Ambepussa Resthouse. One lady very pale and faint with the heat. Sign at Ambipitya, 'Thirst Aid Station'. Cinema in Kandy called 'Wembly'. There are still Hippies in and out of the Buddhist Centre.

*

The retired doctor's story:
    'We were in Paris in 1924. An eminent gynaecologist friend of mine said, "We'll go to Les Grenouilles in Montmarte, perhaps the best restaurant in Paris." But he warned that the proprietor is a law unto himself, and may not admit us even though we have a reservation. Well, we went there and so it proved. My friend went inside but was shortly outside again being pushed and buffeted by the owner. "A reservation! Preposterous! Sacré Bleu! Be off with you!" I cried out, "Oh come on Dr Jean-Paul, let us go elsewhere." My wife, who was with us, was by now nervous. Suddenly, the enraged owner saw my wife, who was, of course, wearing a very fine sari. He cried out, "Wait! Wait!", and rushed back into the restaurant. He came back with champagne and glasses, and begged us to drink. I told my wife in Sinhala, we must do it, in case he became enraged again. She was nervous, but drank. "Now you must dine," and urging us beyond all refusal, he led us into the restaurant where he moved a party already dining and seated

162

us at their table. The dinner was perfect, as only the French know how. And it was all his gift, we paid no bill. Well, after dinner it all came out. He was badly wounded in the First World War, and was about to die on the battlefield when two Indian soldiers found him, and carried him to their doctors, who put him on his feet again. He never forgot the Indian people.'

*

How could one encompass the doctor's non-stop narratives? 'I was in England when Asquith fell, and Lloyd George took over, but I was only a bit of a kid. Lord Athlone, Sir John Bland Sutton [shades of Kipling]. I went through Italy to Venice, Austria, France in the charming company of an Englishman. It was only at Calais that he revealed that he was a don at Magdalen. His brilliant advice, "Wear a national dress as good as your wife's – that wonderful dress she wore at Danielli's – when you go to Oxford."' A romantic Dornford Yatesish Anglo-Sinhalan world, but deep bitterness nonetheless against British Imperialism, and much later against estate dispossession under Mrs B. His old school headmaster – a Jesus man. A Tamil parent complained about our friend's behaviour to this head. 'He said, at once, "You two boys are about the right weight, now you have it out." A ring was formed immediately.

'Travelling through France we met the son of the Mayor of Nice; got on well with him, and travelled some distance in his company. During the course of this companionship he said to my wife, "That is the most beautiful ring you have on your finger. Sell it to me, and on my proceeds you can have a wonderful time in France." My wife, who is a very nervous woman, said, "I intend to have a wonderful time in France, *and* keep my ring."'

*

The coucals in the dahlias. So close that their backs reveal a covering of blue and black good enough for an emperor's

163

head. But in this setting they are not Firbank, only a mirage in
suburban Surrey.

*

The doctor (a staunch UNP man) had obviously been very rich
and well connected. Yet, during British days it was many
moons before he received an invitation to the British Club. And
then he refused because his wife was not invited as well. Good
for him! Someone told me that the swimming pool of the British
Club was still not open to the Singhalese for some years *after*
independence.

*

A small boy on the bank of the Nuwarawewa Tank at
Anuradhapura. 'Many fish in the tank. Over there Dagoba,
Lord Buddha. Over there, Hindu Temple. Lord Hindu, sir. I
am making a collection of small coins [one given]. Also my
brother is doing it.' No more coins given.

*

Fourteen-year-old student by the Tank, 'Your country very
good for poor people. Co-operative shops, starting in village of
Rochdale.'

*

Tiny girl, in knickers only, running from her house near the
holy city at Anuradhapura when she saw us, shouting,
'Bum-bum!' Followed by an older sister, shouting, 'Bon-
bon!'

*

I suddenly remembered (why?) Robert's tale of being tested by
his employer's wife – money under the carpet. He saw the catch
at once, but took it philosophically (not the money!). This took
me back to the old women of Felsham in Suffolk when I judged

their painted egg competition. Every one of them had been tested in the same way when they were in service. There aren't many domestic servants left in Suffolk.

*

Snake birds fly overhead, but I am getting down to work. T. is a hard taskmaster.

*

Monk at the very early Dagoba was amazed at our offer of money for the Temple, when we refused his offer to guide us. He was almost exactly like Francis Wormald. Another man appeared, and walked with us. Formerly a policeman, on duty one night when a drunk comes in; tells him to bugger off, but sergeant informs against him for not arresting the man. He is dismissed; three children. Major Sarson, visiting Anuradhapura, but can do nothing (although he had been in charge there in British days). Still can't make up his mind whether he should blame the major or not.

*

Very jolly free-enterprise lady gets into conversation. Adores Far Eastern nylon saris. She *can* get them from smugglers, but it is complicated. Car ride, then bus, then marsh walk (as though to enjoy countryside), into an old woman's hut, where saris are packed into the bottom of a bag and then covered with cardboard. The bag is then concealed under two petticoats. The walk back to the bus is very slow, but dignified. This is essential.

*

Ceylon hounds, proud gingerish-coloured pointers. They are ubiquitous. The most immovable of all creatures on the road, impervious to hooting. Their high bark ends in a moan-like noise – Sybil Thorndike in *Saint Joan*.

*

Kalpitiya, seventeenth-century Dutch fort with ten-mile underground tunnel to the sea – full of bat dung. Very smelly.

*

In every village chillis spread out to dry on the road. Startling red, but depressing to think of how much good food is ruined by their use in cooking.

*

Elegance of men and women. A high proportion of strikingly handsome and beautiful men, women, and children. Great contrast to the ugly, plain, and ill-dressed tourists.

*

We were put down on the bill of a remote resthouse as: 'Mr and Miss Ancos Willsin.' (About right too, was the comment of our travel agent when we got back to the UK.)

*

Wilapattu Jungle Reserve. Our bungalow was twenty-seven miles into the jungle. It was wonderful, though even then anxiety and despair lurked in the undergrowth and trailed from the trees. In the early morning outing, six to eight a.m. especially, great fatigue, numbness. What does one await with eagle, leopard, boar, deer, mongoose, even tortoise – the watching of movements, shape etc. when it's unaware or at the moment of recognition? – both, I think, but the crocodile's eye one never meets, nor the monitor's.

*

Depression of death of the jungle itself: intense competition for life by plants and animals and, in the near future probably, encroachment by man as the great Mahaweli Ganga irrigation scheme gets under way in the dry area. Poachers have always encroached. Though I suspect that there is much less 'big game hunting' in Sri Lanka than in Africa or India.

*

It is so dramatic forcing one's way (in fact bumping madly in a jeep on a rutted sand track) through the jungle. Then suddenly there is a great lake with bright green grass at the edges like an artificial lake at an English country house. And, if you're lucky, there is a bear digging his holes.

*

A passing tourist jeep – the drivers always stop for the trackers to exchange information about sightings and so forth. Anyway they have to stop to let pass, as the tracks are all single. In the other jeep a French lady complaining bitterly, 'Rien à voir! Rien à voir!', because they hadn't seen a leopard. That day we saw seventeen varieties of birds, a jackal, sambhur deer, mongeese, spotted deer, a monitor lizard, tortoises, crocodiles, mouse deer, langhur monkeys and leopard tracks.

*

We had an exceptional tracker. 'I do not have many English words to describe this, sir. But I came to Wilapattu as a boy, and I knew that this was the place I must care for.' He had no folksy tales like European guides, no Walt Disneyish whimsicality about the animals; no speculation; always admitting lack of knowledge (which was seldom). The trackers are brave men. Three killed in that reserve by poachers. Of the animals, the most dangerous for them are elephants, and bears. The latter are particularly dangerous when their heads are buried in ant-hills and then they panic upon sudden awareness of human beings.

*

In the jungle continuous daytime call of barbets (very difficult to see them); the call is a cross between the cry of a cuckoo and the clucking of a hen. There are spasmodic cries of hawk eagles, babblers, and bee-eaters. Then sudden loud din of malabar pied hornbill, which Salim Ali describes in his book of Indian birds as 'a variety of loud raucous cackling and inane screams reminiscent of the protestations of a dak bungalow murghi seized by the cook'. This exactly describes it for me, even though I am not sure what he means.

*

Car breakdown on the road to Jaffna, luckily in a village where many willing hands help to push. T. feels naked without a word of the local language, but his nakedness is nothing to my complete lack of clothes. Their kindness is equal to our foolishness. Only two other private cars during the next sixty miles to Jaffna.

*

I have a cold.

*

As we drive into Jaffna, the Tamil high hedge screens to their houses take me back to my novel *As If By Magic* and to Kipling's house in Vermont.

*

Our Jaffna guide, Michael, tells me Tamil writers are all upcountry tea-estate Indians, not locals.

*

I remember a previous visit in 1970 seeing that the only British authors on sale were Hall Caine and Marie Corelli. Michael says that now there is plenty of James Hadley Chase.

*

I am reminded of Barbara Cartland in Udaipur at the Maharajah's lake palace (now a hotel). The receptionist was very proud of her visit: 'We had very important lady here, sir. Cartland Barbara.' I suggested that the name should be the other way round. He was adamant. 'No, sir. See here in the registration book, "Cartland Barbara".' Then, 'Later on we were greatly favoured by a visit from Cartland Barbara's son.'

*

Sea eagles far overhead as I write some novel notes on the roof of the hotel. But cold worse, nose dripping, and v. slight temperature. Michael arrives. Gives us Tamil phrases in exchange for French which he is learning. He tells me, 'Si vous êtes si malade, pourquoi n'êtes vous pas chez vous.' It did not become that serious, luckily. He has no Sinhala, but very good English.

*

At breakfast in the hotel a little girl screams at the sight of me and cannot be calmed by her parents. She is removed by the mother. Later she appeared on the hotel roof where I was writing. From the scattered toys it was clearly a playroom of hers. Violent screams again and her nurse rushed out to remove her. She was obviously horrified at the sight of the ogre again, and in the panic of retreat her little shoes fell off and lay pathetically overturned on the floor. All this did not help my writing confidence: I love small children and they usually love me. Michael, when he arrived, found it all very funny; but then he was worried when I told him that popular Princess Pat Ramsay and Mary, Queen of Scots were loved by dogs and children. Later, the girl's father came to apologize: it seems that my white hair had made the girl think of Father Christmas, and as Christmas was over, it was unseasonable and frightening of FC to appear again.

It made me feel older, and fell in with my spoken and unspoken emphasis on being old (serves me right), because apart from financial worry and tummy pains I do not feel old at all.

*

Swedish couple (I had seen them earlier in the Hindu Temple) fussing about the wickedness of lovely natural fish being fried. To frowns because it is all so cheap for tourists in Sri Lanka and must be supremely cheap for them. But I am annoyed because everyone in the hotel is 'doing their best' (although there are silly muddles). Young American at the next table says, 'I just send it back until it comes as I want it. That's the American method.' Is my fury because I am totally cut off from money-making and efficiency? I want some elementary things – three cups of tea for breakfast. I believe it easier to think that all good things come by chance.

*

With Michael on the Causeway. A meeting with a Moslem merchant and his large family. Michael is amazed at my easy social intercourse, and for him, a Tamil Catholic, social dealings with a Moslem are astounding. His eyes are twice the size throughout the whole encounter, which extended into an invitation, first, to the merchant's local Mosque, and to his home. Michael had never been into a Mosque before – his eyes were three times their usual size. The merchant and fellow merchants who had by then joined us were amazed when we said that in many Islamic countries it would be forbidden for us to accompany them into the Mosque. 'But that is un-believable, sir. You are welcome into this Mosque as into my home. We are Tamil Moslems, not Arabs. In the Koran, we are told that Mohammed tells a Christian priest to use the Mosque.' Michael shakes his head in amazed disbelief. We are courteously entertained in his house; but his wife, who appeared to be behind a curtain, did not come out to greet us.

*

We are invited to dinner in a Tamil household (there was total disbelief from our Singhalese friends when we returned to the South). A little boy of fourteen (who looks to be eight) runs the whole meal with great efficiency. His bad behaviour in his own family has led to his being an outcast from them.

*

With Michael we take the ferry across to the north-westernmost islands. A gentleman who is an agricultural salesman says they have new crops such as chewing tobacco. Where should they seek an export market? Apart from an old man in Rose, Texas, who spat across my path, I couldn't recall when I'd last seen a man chewing. The salesman knew that Parvathi was the wife of Siva, and he had been to Mahabilipuram and Conjeeveram. He tells a nearby old man of our brief discussion of Hinduism, whereupon the old man immediately abases himself before me – I must be a Holy Man (damn that white hair). The other ferry passengers are torn between giggles and serious attention.

*

A slender young engineer at a sacred pool, looks so like a poet at a party. He talks very fast, and tells many legends about the mongoose-faced Chula princess, but always follows his stories with, 'it may be true, it may be false; people are always asking.' I suggest that it may be a mystery, and he seizes this word with ecstatic delight, and repeats it over and over again.

*

The Prime Minister's party has promised to erect a statue to a Tamil boy who was killed by the police in recent riots. In the hinterland, a statue of another local Tamil hero hangs by its metal stanchions, head down; the police dragged it from its pedestal.

*

The Commission looking into the recent riots is meeting in

171

the enormous Moghul-style Public Library. It was all built in 1954, and has a Hindu God (? the Goddess of Wisdom) outside.

*

At the Siva Temple. An elegant approach to the Sanctuary. Doric columns and bulbous Belgian-made glass lamps. Five minutes of music from the band, then Siva is exposed. Then the same ceremony at the side of the Temple. Devotees hitting the sides of their heads with clenched fists, then crossing their arms and reaching up to grasp the lobes of their ears whilst bending their knees three times. It is all over very quickly, much to the relief of Michael and T.

*

Saint James Catholic Church, December 25th 1976. Two policemen making fun of two Tamil men who reacted by kicking the police. Eight policemen then arrived and beat up the congregration, blood everywhere. Michael's account is passionate and bitter. Now many more Tamil policemen are employed locally, whereas before they were all Singhalese. Perhaps this was a version of 'divide and rule' – older Sri Lankans never cease to accuse the British of this policy. The Church roof is supported by pillars in the Hindu style.

*

Small girl in Jaffna town persistently kisses our feet whilst asking for money. An old man gives her a great bang in order to insert himself into the receiving position.

*

Jaffna Archaeological Museum. A fine painting of Queen Victoria in splendid gilt frame with elephant supports. It was given by the Queen to the loyal people of Jaffna in 1853. Astrologer's palanquin last used in 1900. Good engraving of the Fort in 1760: in the foreground landscape several Dutch officials in full, heavy, eighteenth-century costume. They must have been very hot.

*

Very good seafood at the Kankisanturi Resthouse on the northern coast. Town locally known as KKS, rather like Totters for Tottenham Court Road. The food made me think of the best of Sri Lankan dishes: smoked seer fish, buffalo curd with jaggery (brown sugar), omelettes, prawns (when you can get those which haven't been exported to Singapore), paw-paw (though there is too much of it, and it does taste, oddly, of petrol), mangosteens, small bananas, pineapples. The puddings of the old British days seem to have disappeared unlike India where queen's pudding and treacle sponge abound.

*

Last time I was in Jaffna I bought several scented swan-design fans made of straw, and yesterday I said loudly for the fifth time in the hotel that I really must see if they were still obtainable: there was no response from anyone. Today, I took time off from writing, and discovered some fans in the town and brought them back triumphantly to the hotel. The large lady receptionist said, 'Ah! Good! So at last you have got a fanny. You have been asking for one every day. And now you are happy!'

*

Frogs on bathroom wall of Resthouse, backing up and down like Kandyan dancers. The servant boy confided, 'Tourist ladies not liking frogs, going up or down.'

*

Sri Lankan Minister of Transport questioned in Parliament over his purchase of Romanian-built railway carriages. Many complaints received that the seats are so close that lady

173

passengers are embarrassed as their legs continually knock against those of other passengers.

*

Strong political feeling in Sri Lanka that she and other allies were badly neglected by the winning powers after the war because of massive aid to Germany and Japan. 'Sri Lanka must now take a leaf out of Germany's book and pull herself together as Germany did largely by her own efforts.' And the new Prime Minister, Jayawardene, increasingly looks towards Japan as a natural ally.

*

I don't know whether to be cheered or not by the sister of a Singhalese friend, 'Mr Angus has a face that tells me he went to a good school.'

*

Overheard in the Intercontinental Hotel, Colombo: 'He was at prep school with me – Heath Mount. I haven't seen him in forty years. He went to Dartmouth. His brother was an old Murchistonian. Lorry went over him. Nothing much left.'

*

The theme of my novel constantly returning to my *Sunday Times* children's story – big room, etc., child and grandmother.

*

T. tries to make telephone call from the Tourist Hotel: several coins when inserted went right through the machine at the bottom and fell to the floor; he was cut off six times in the middle of conversation; always completely cut off at the end of 25 cents' worth of call; often cut off before the call had begun; line repeatedly engaged; telephone situated under stairs next to staff toilets and in passage leading to swimming pool; constant clatter of heavy German tourists in wood shoes; no ventilation.

*

Overheard in Intercontinental Hotel, Colombo:

Young Japanese businessman – 'Colombo, too many people, very polluted!'

Sri Lankan businessman – 'But Tokyo is having pollution and people problems?'

Young Japanese businessman – 'No. Now Japan very strong regulation stopping motor-car exhaustion.'

*

Coachload of German tourists standing by the bank of the Dutch canal, north of Colombo, photographing Sri Lankan women washing themselves in the water. I wonder if the tourists would welcome Sri Lankan women into *their* homes to take photos of *them* having a bath?

Arizona
1984

*

    *   *

   *

To have spent four months in Arizona and to have missed seeing the Grand Canyon and nearly all the Indian Reservations sounds odd, I know. The failure to see the Canyon is easily explained – vertigo. My vertigo is so strong that I even feel dizzy stepping out of my automobile. A high-born anglophile American friend of mine left off praising England to urge that on no account should I miss the Canyon. I said that I might fly over. No, he said, you must walk round the rim. Well, I raised the issue with a gentleman in a Tucson bar. He said he often used to go with his second wife who taught him how to get the most fabulous view by leaning over the rim. He said he owed that and a lot more to her before she passed away.

But I knew, long before I set out, that I should have to settle for other pleasures in Arizona, and I can assure fellow vertigo sufferers that there are many wonders apart from the Canyon. But I am sad not to have seen more of the Indian Reservations. I caught a glimpse of the Navajo Reservation when visiting the Little Painted Desert (which is as exciting as the Great Painted Desert, and you can't see it from the Interstate). The distant mesas of the Reservation looked very wild and strange. Tony Hillerman's Navajo tribal police heroes are remarkably sensitive to that countryside, and wonderfully evocative descriptions abound in his detective novels. But I saw hardly anything myself, the reason being that I was a Visiting Professor at the University of Arizona, and could only travel at weekends.

Arizona is a big State. I even failed, owing to my teaching duties, to attend the lecture on the Indian Oral Tradition in literature, by the famous U of A Indian professor, N. Scott Momaday.

*

By being based at Tucson in the South of the State, I was in the heart of the Sonoran Desert, the giant Saguaro cactus country which respects no border and runs far into Mexico. As a sun-lover, I was happy, but the apparently barren desert was oppressive after a while. Thus I was cheered on a visit North to Phoenix to see, near Casa Grande and Eloy, cotton fields and citrus orchards. But those who know the desert would find this stupid. They know just how much animal and plant life thrives in the desert. The remarkable Sonora Desert Museum outside Tucson proves them right. I was in the desert in the Fall, but photographs show a staggering blaze of colour over the desert floor after Spring rain. March snow here in England, as I write, suggests that I am not living wisely.

*

Apart from the Desert Museum, the other two great features of Tucson are the University, whose elegant palm-lined Mall stretches widely East and West. And, hard by the town, the eighteenth-century Franciscan Baroque church of St Xavier del Bac, white and massive, rises as successor to the seventeenth-century Padre Kino Jesuit mission church.

The Hispanic and Indian feeling of the town and the whole area, the humming birds, the sunsets are not America if you half-close your eyes. A friend, an Indian from India, poet on the Campus, stopped outside the restaurant where we were about to eat, and exclaimed, as he looked at the sunset and smelt drifting woodsmoke, 'Oh, I am in Delhi!'

The Catalinas to the North, the Tucson Mountains to the West, and the Rincons to the East have prevented the greedy eating-up of the desert so apparent at Phoenix. There is only one Interstate, so the town has an air of calm. But, incredibly and unbelievably, the landing flight path of the Davis-Monthan air base lies North West-South East right across the town. The incoming flights shatter University study and retired peace, as well as being potentially very dangerous.

But culture survives the impact of the war machine. Apart from three first-class bookstores, there is a long-established and flourishing Poetry Centre. You can get real coffee at Bentley's (not the usual see-through American coffee) and hear Rameau on the harpsicord while you drink it. You can see a production of that very rude play, Cloud 9, and you can cheer that the U of A is the only University in the States to have sacrificed a football practice field for a library extension.

There is still some feeling of the Old West, however. We cruised for a parking space, and a police officer asked what we were up to. Tony, who drives for me, said, 'I am looking for a vacant space.' The police officer yelled, 'Well, why don't you use your head!' He was so pleased with his quip that he fired off a couple of rounds from his gun. A student T-shirt legend echoed his gunfire: 'God, Guns, and Guts.' But a bumper sticker showed that there were other attitudes: 'Have you hugged a Homosexual Today?'

There was fine enterprise, too, in the town: special gloves to keep your hands clean when reading the *New York Times*, and 'hominy grits for your Persian cat'. Oddest, perhaps, was the flashing invitation to 'Join Our Exotic Girls in the Cactus Garden', a prickly event I avoided.

*

At Phoenix, the mountains are further away, hence the town's enormous spread. But much of it is elegant and, where there are Frank Lloyd Wright buildings, distinguished. But will there be enough water ahead for those lovely lawns? When you wade through several miles of suburbs and reach the gates of Taliesin West, one knows that it was worth the ride, but wishes that Lloyd Wright's influence had been greater on the design of the houses which now reach to the gates of his ranch. FLW detail is everywhere evident, and immediately, for the very Estate gate is unquestionably 'Wright'. You enter another world.

The building itself doesn't quite live up to the most usually seen photograph, but the sensitivity to nature, to the desert and the ingenuity of design is vastly impressive throughout. Could I live as a student in the Community? No. A writer needs psychological air. Anyway, no-one invited me to join.

*

We left refreshed and lunched at the Arizona Biltmore Resort Inn, where Wrightian interior detail is exciting and pervasive. We had a very good lunch, enlivened by a Republican at the next table (it was Election time). He was impressing upon his guests the dangers of a Democratic victory: 'How could people from the Carter-Mondale era have any idea how to handle the worst deficit we've ever had?'

Back to our comfortable motel to recover, but we were a little put out by the strict guest rules: 'Please do not enter the pool during the cleaning process, and do not interfere with the service man.' Whatever can have happened?

*

Out of Phoenix and on North West over the White Mountains, where two blue birds crossed our path. The remote wildness was a romantic preparation for the amazing Petrified Forest, and the no less astounding Painted Desert. Had there been time, the Reservations lay before us. . . .

There *was* just time to see the twelfth-century Montezuma Castle. Water ran fast through the creek, overshadowed by giant sycamore trees, and watched over by the cliff dwellings. It was peaceful and impressive. Had time allowed it would have been interesting to have stopped at nearby Arcosanti, to compare Soleri's new urban architecture with the early Indian work.

Startling artefacts – the exquisitely elegant Navajo rugs, and the wild turquoise jewellery – pounded my sight and mind, which was already reeling from the impact of the outlandish colours and forms of nature. As I left Arizona, I felt with the poet, Richard Shelton:

'Living in the desert,
Has taught me to go inside myself for shade.'